EASTERN MONTANA

A Portrait of
The Land and Its People

NUMBER 2

MONTANA GEOGRAPHIC SERIES

BY JOHN A. ALWIN
Associate Professor of Geography
Department of Earth Sciences
Montana State University

Published By

MONTANA MAGAZINE, INC.

Helena, Montana

Rick Graetz, Publisher
Mark Thompson, Editor
Carolyn Cunningham, Managing Editor

PREFACE

To many, Montana is synonymous with mountains. For the western third of the state there could be no more appropriate name. The first volume in this series elegantly illustrates the mountainous splendor that is western Montana. But there is another Montana. Its land and people are the topic of this portrait.

Eastern Montana is a land of sweeping vistas and seemingly endless expanses stretching to the horizon. It is a big country, an open country, and perhaps no other section of the state is more deserving of the Big Sky label. This is home to the Missouri Breaks, Fort Peck, Bighorn Canyon, mountain outliers, badlands and pine parklands. It is Old West country, the land of the Cheyenne and Crow, where Custer fought and died, where cowboys, Calamity Jane and Kid Curry add to the regional mystique. Striped grain fields and fenced range now prevail where buffalo once grazed.

Some say this is where much of Montana's future lies. It is a region rich in energy and food production at a time when the world is clamoring for more of both. Already home to half of Montana's population, it also claims the state's two largest urban areas in Billings and Great Falls.

And yet, even for many Montanans, it may be the most misunderstood section of the state, perhaps in part because it has not received the same amount of widespread exposure as its western counterpart. It is a place that merits closer inspection by residents and nonresidents alike. Those who take the time to look will discover an Eastern Montana with its own character and pride, unpretentious and honest — the real thing. Those who take the time to look will find a big chunk of what makes Montana such a special place.

John A. Alwin
Bozeman, Montana

ACKNOWLEDGMENTS

The following Montana State University associates graciously agreed to review sections of this book:

Dr. Joe Ashley, Associate Professor of Geography; Dr. Merrill Burlingame, Professor Emeritus of History; Prof. Paul Dawson, Assistant Professor of Atmospheric Science; Prof. M. J. Edie, Professor of Geography; Dr. Michael Hager, Director, Museum of the Rockies; Dr. James Heimbach, Research Associate, Institute of Natural Resources; Dr. John Montagne, Professor of Geology; Dr. Tom Roll, Associate Professor of Anthropology; Dr. M. Douglas Scott, Director, Institute of Natural Resources.

John Alwin

John Alwin

Rick Graetz

John Alwin

Montana Magazine Inc., Publisher
Box 5630, Helena, Mt. 59604

ISBN 0-938314-02-5

John Alwin

Montana Travel Promotion Unit

John Alwin

Contents

PART I

EASTERN MONTANA: THE LAND

GREAT PLAINS MONTANA

Driving the highways of Montana, don't expect to cross a wide yellow line and see a road sign announcing: "You Are Now Entering Eastern Montana."

One reason for the lack of demarcation is that the limits of Eastern Montana vary depending on who's defining it and what criteria are being used. The region could be based on climate, topography, vegetation, aboriginal inhabitants, historical development, economic factors or many other variables, each of which would suggest different boundaries. In addition each Montanan probably has a unique notion of the extent of the region. Few would object to the inclusion of the area immediately west of the North and South Dakota state lines in an Eastern Montana region, but how far west does Eastern Montana extend? Miles City, Wolf Point and Glasgow are obviously in the east, Thompson Falls, Kalispell and Missoula are clearly western, but how about Browning, Helena, White Sulphur Springs, Lewistown or Big Timber? Where would you place the contact between east and west in Montana and what would be the basis for your division?

For many, Eastern Montana evidently starts where the mountains end and the plains begin. Max Bloom of Lewistown said he thinks his community is on the border, "because the mountains start here." Likewise, Lois Woodard, owner-operator of the Roy Grocery, said she believes the dividing lines passes through a point 12 miles east of Roy. "This is right where the mountains end," she said. Smoot Rowley, a 55-year resident of Choteau, considers himself an Eastern Montanan since he lives "on the beginning of the prairie and open country." Even nonresident Robert Thorpe, long-time train attendant on the Empire Builder serving Montana's Hi-Line, bases contact between east and west on topography. He senses he is leaving Eastern Montana behind when he feels the train straining as it starts up the slope west of Cut Bank.

Western Montanans who have had limited firsthand contact with Eastern Montana may think of it as a dry, flat, desolate and monotonous expanse dominated by sameness and plainness out east of the mountains, where it is extremely cold in the winter or excessively hot in the summer.

A recent survey of Montanans from both east and west suggests that many residents have a distorted image of the eastern section of their state. Western Montanans who have had limited firsthand contact with the area may think of it as a dry, flat, desolate and monotonous expanse dominated by sameness and plainness out east of the mountains, where it is either extremely cold in the winter or excessively hot in the summer. Residents of the area with their greater intimacy and knowledge of Eastern Montana's beauty and variety take opposition to what they would say are misconceptions about their region.

John Rickard, a 21-year resident of Eastern Montana, seems to echo the feeling of many of his neighbors when he proclaims, "Eastern Montana has a hidden beauty equal to the panoramic beauty of the West. That beauty is harder to see, more subtle to the eye — the antelope moving across the grasslands, the gorges and gullies with their small rivers and streams, and green life struggling to survive the heat of summer or the icy blast of the winter winds. Eastern Montana is a land that looks barren to a foreigner, but holds many beauties to the native." Lifetime Ashland resident, Gerry Robinson puts it this way: "Eastern Montana has a great variety of scenery and landscapes that range from lofty mountain tops to areas that resemble a desert. The mountain tops are quite a bit further apart, but when you're on one, you're on top of the world!"

Montana is a state with a dual physiographic personality — Rocky Mountain Montana in the western third and Great Plains Montana to the east. The North American Great Plains province extends from southern Texas northward through Eastern Montana and on into Canada. The United States portion covers about 450,000 square miles and lies between the Rocky Mountains on the west and the Central Lowlands to the east. Although the surface of the Great Plains slopes gently eastward and drops about 3,000 feet between the base of the Rocky Mountains and its eastern boundary, it is not without significant regional variations. This is especially true in Eastern Montana.

Opposite: *Where the Plains meet the mountains.* — George Wuerthner

Great Plains Montana begins at the foot of the Northern Rockies at an elevation of about 5,000 feet and slopes gradually to the east. This surface is only about 2,000 feet above sea level at the North Dakota line. Although the horizontal dimension is pervasive over this plains area, the topography is rarely flat. Mountains spill over into the plains, and deeply entrenched rivers, buttes, and areas of badlands and rugged breaks all add variety to the region's lines. In fact, Eastern Montana falls within the Missouri Plateau, one of the most rugged portions of the Great Plains.

WESTERN MONTANANS LOOK TO THE EAST

"From an airplane, it (Eastern Montana) begins where my eyes wander from the window to a magazine in my lap."

"When it snows in Eastern Montana, it blows rather than coming down straight."

"The West is used for recreation, the East is used for work."

"A good place to find antelope and jackrabbits."

"Being from Whitefish, I always assumed Eastern Montana was on the other side of Glacier National Park."

"The East is more of a treeless dry area."

"I applied for a job in Shelby; I've never been there. I hope it's not perfectly flat."

Our Eastern Montana includes all of the state's Great Plains area plus the Bighorn and Pryor mountains section. In a strict physiographic sense these latter two highlands belong within the Rocky Mountain province. Physiography aside, however, these always have been a part of Eastern Montana to its people. Their aboriginal inhabitants were members of the plains culture group and today this part of southcentral Montana is perceived to be eastern by state residents. Most tend to draw their contact between east and west further to the west, through the Red Lodge area.

Top: *Arrow River from Square Butte, Little Belt Mountains in the distance.* — Jim Romo

Bottom: *The Missouri's last few miles in Montana. This shot taken where state Highway 16 crosses the river near Culbertson.* — Mark Thompson

BENEATH THE PLAINS

The horizontal dimension dominates over most of Eastern Montana and can be linked directly to the generally flat underlying rock units. The geologic history associated with Eastern Montana is a fascinating one. Its rocks tell a story of times when large seas innundated the area, when lush subtropical swamps were commonplace, and when dinosaurs or camels were the norm.

If we go back about 75 million years to the Cretaceous Period, we can consider some of the geologic factors that helped shape this region and produce rocks we now see at and near the surface. By at least that time, mountain-building forces had caused the Rocky Mountains to begin rising above adjacent areas from Alaska to Central America. As the Rockies rose in western Montana, a narrow and shallow seaway which cut North America in two, began to close. The western shoreline of this Cretaceous sea lapped up on the eastern flank of the evolving Rockies and fluctuated east and west in response to the mountain building to the west and sinking of the seafloor itself. When the sea advanced westward, marine mud accumulated over what was then the ocean floor of Eastern Montana. Retreats of the sea are recorded in non-marine land deposits, including sands which had been eroded from the rising western highland. Transported seaward by Cretaceous rivers, sand was deposited in deltas and on coastal plains. Other material came to rest in continental lagoons, swamps and shallow lakes on the emergent land west of the seaway. These sedimentary deposits accumulated in essentially flat-lying layers which eventually totaled thousands of feet in thickness. In succeeding millions of years, the deposits hardened, the muds becoming shale; the sands, sandstone; and some of the swampy organic debris, coal.

Fossils and bones in these late Cretaceous rocks tell us that life thrived both on the land and in the sea. Remains of warm temperate and subtropical plants such as palms, ferns, and fig trees attest to a much milder and more equable climate than we have today. Coal deposits dating from this period suggest the existence of near-coastal swamps similar to today's Florida Everglades.

Perhaps the most celebrated residents of late Cretaceous Eastern Montana were the great dinosaurs, which dominated the land, and the marine lizards, which ruled the sea. According to Dr. Michael W. Hager, vertebrate paleontologist and director of the Museum of the Rockies in Bozeman, "Eastern Montana is clearly one of the most important regions in the world for the excavation and research on the last of the dinosaurs." Extraordinary finds have been made and paleontologists continue to comb the region, excavating known dig areas and searching for new ones. Around the small town of Jordan, the annual summer arrival of a crew of paleontologists from the University of California at Berkeley, locally referred to as the bone diggers, is now a tradition.

"Eastern Montana is clearly one of the most important regions in the world for excavation and research on the last of the dinosaurs."

Above: *Excavation at this site near Lindsay unearthed 11,000-year-old mammoth remains that evidently had been scavenged by early hunters. The animal and interpretive material are on display at the Museum of the Rockies in Bozeman. —* Courtesy Leslie B. Davis

Bottom: *MORT, so named for the Museum of the Rockies Triceratops, being cast in plaster to protect it for the journey to the museum in Bozeman where it is on display. —* Museum of the Rockies

> Few at the time even speculated that such a creature ever had lived, but here was the world's first proof, lying just beneath the surface outside Jordan, Montana.

In 1902 an earlier fossil-hunting team working in a section of Garfield County north of Jordan, made a discovery that startled the scientific world. The expedition was from the American Museum in New York City, its leader was noted dinosaur collector Barnum Brown, and their discovery was something that no scientist had ever seen — the remains of the largest carnivore ever to have walked the earth. This was *Tyrannosaurus rex*, the "King of the tyrant lizards." Few at the time even speculated that such a creature ever had lived, but here was the world's first proof, lying just beneath the surface outside Jordan, Montana. One skeleton would have sufficed, but Brown's party unearthed two excellent specimens!

Each of Brown's creatures probably weighed eight tons when alive, and measured more than 40 feet long. Upright they carried their massive heads almost 20 feet above the ground. Their powerful four-foot long jaws were equipped with dozens of dagger-like, serrated teeth up to six inches long. Eight-inch talons on each of their six toes added to the creatures' battle array, although there are now dinosaur experts who challenge their ferocious, monster-movie image. Some believe that the beasts may have been too slow to have been active predators and may have had to rely on carrion. The debate continues.

To date, only four American museums have, or are now preparing, upright *Tyrannosaurus* skeletons. The American Museum in New York City and the Carnegie Museum in Pittsburgh each has one of the original discovery skeletons unearthed by Barnum Brown. In 1968 the Los Angeles County Museum acquired another Garfield County *Tyrannosaurus* which has since been mounted. In the summer of 1981, an expedition headed by Dr. Michael Hager of the Museum of the Rockies unearthed bones of yet another *Tyrannosaurus* in badlands 50 miles northeast of Jordan. The Museum soon will have only the fourth mounted *Tyrannosaurus* in the country.

Although *Tyrannosaurus* may have held center stage in Eastern Montana's late Cretaceous landscape, other dinosaurs shared the coastal plains. One was *Triceratops*, with its distinctive bony frill and three long horns, one above each eye and the other on the nose. Thirty feet long and weighing up to 10 tons, it was the largest of the horned dinosaurs. Evidence suggests it may have been the prey of *Tyrannosaurus*. The late Cretaceous Hell Creek Sandstone also has yielded remains of other dinosaurs, including duck-billed dinosaurs. Up to 25 feet long, these herbivores probably frequented shallow water areas where they fed on swamp vegetation. Unable to fend off the large carnivores of the time, they probably sought refuge in deep water.

While *Tyrannosaurus*, *Triceratops*, the duck-billed, and other dinosaurs dominated animal life on the land, giant reptiles went unchallenged in the adjacent sea. The most intimidating of these marine lizards may well have been the streamlined *Mosasaurus*, 30-foot-long creatures not unlike the sea serpents of mythology. Bones of these carnivores have been found beneath the famous Hell Creek formation.

While Eastern Montana's giant dinosaurs and marine reptiles may hold the greatest interest for the general public, other recent finds continue to excite experts.

Discoveries made in the vicinity of the south shore of Fort Peck Reservoir in the early 1960s, near what is now known as the Bug Creek site, drew widespread notice among paleontologists. Researchers unearthed thousands of mammalian teeth and jaw fragments, and the remains of fish, amphibians and reptiles. Included was a wide variety of animals, such as pike, sturgeon, ray, crocodile, alligator, turtle, frog, oppossum and aquatic bird species, as well as late Cretaceous dinosaurs and lizards. Also discovered were previously undescribed mammals, which have led to a rethinking of the accepted model of mammalian evolution.

The 1964 discovery of *Deinonychus*, the "terrible claw," is considered one of the world's most important dinosaur finds in decades. Discovered in early Cretaceous rocks outside Bridger, this nine-foot-long creature with a long, rigid tail which was held out horizontally, stood on two powerful back legs and was only about four feet tall. Lightly built and carnivorous, it was apparently extremely agile. As its name implies, one of its most distinctive features was a five-inch-long claw attached to a third toe. It was held above the ground and was used exclusively for tearing open prey. Fundamentally different than other dinosaur discoveries, *Deinonychus* lends credence to an ongoing argument against the traditional view of all dinosaurs as lethargic, cold-blooded reptiles.

Eastern Montana was again in the dinosaur limelight in 1979. That summer, outside Choteau, a Princeton University paleontologist discovered a nest containing 15 baby duck-billed dinosaurs along with eggshell fragments and several complete eggs. Conditions conducive to the preservation of dinosaur eggs for 60 million years rarely are met, and eggs have been found in only a few other locations in the world.

By approximately 70 million years ago, the age of dinosaurs was waning and all species would be extinct by the end of the period. Their disappearance in Eastern Montana and worldwide is still a mystery. Explanations range from climatic change to disease, and from cataclysmic celestial events to competition with mammals. With the story of the last of the dinosaurs recorded in its late Cretaceous rocks, Eastern Montana undoubtedly will figure largely in the quest to understand the extinction of these noble beasts.

Over the eastern half of Great Plains Montana late Cretaceous strata are covered by sedimentary rocks deposited during the succeeding Tertiary Period, which includes the span of time from about 65,000,000 to 1,000,000 years ago. These younger rocks were once more extensive, but later erosion removed many of these deposits from western sections of Eastern Montana and, to the good fortune of dinosaur hunters, exposed the underlying, older Cretaceous age rocks. All Tertiary deposits were non-marine. Dominant layers are shale, sandstone and coal. Most were deposited by slow moving streams that meandered back and forth across a broad and very gently sloping plain extending eastward from the still rising Rockies.

The oldest Tertiary deposit is the Fort Union formation. It developed at a time when warm and moist conditions dominated the low plains of Eastern Montana. Extensive swampy areas and associated standing water provided ideal conditions for the accumulation of organic debris, the necessary raw material for coal formations. Today this is the chief coal bearing unit in the entire Northern Great Plains and is mined extensively in Montana, Wyoming and North Dakota. Following the early Tertiary, Eastern Montana's climate became drier, and by the end of the period the region was a cooler, grass-covered plain similar to what it is today. Layers of interbedded volcanic ash are proof of Tertiary volcanic activity to the west.

Above: *Interesting erosional shapes in a road cut north of Culbertson.* — John Alwin

Below: *Swamps from some 65 to 55 million years ago account for Montana's famous Ft. Union coal formation shown here at Decker.*

Above: *The red in many Eastern Montana roads comes from the use of clinker for resurfacing.* — Jim Romo

Below: *An unusually deep seam of clinker, some 75 feet thick, along the Tongue River.* — Bob Chadwick

As with the Cretaceous age rocks, Eastern Montana Tertiary sediments also have proved to be a veritable treasure chest for paleontologists, providing valuable insight into mammalian evolution. Remains of mammals ranging from small rodents to the diminutive, foot-tall *Eohippus*, the "dawn horse;" the primitive ungulate, *Coryphodon*; early camels; rhinoceroses; and mammoths catalog the ascendence of mammals over Eastern Montana during the Tertiary Period.

Where not completely removed by erosion, Tertiary sediments and even some Cretaceous deposits commonly develop a dense drainage network and classic badlands topography. These deposits usually are composed of relatively clay-rich shales, mudstones and ashes and are therefore unable to absorb much rainfall. Runoff is thus shed quickly. An intricate network of interconnected gullies soon develops in the usually loosely consolidated and weak underlying sediments, producing a contorted, badlands topography. A concentration of rainfall in widely scattered showers and little vegetative cover accelerates this type of erosion.

CLINKER
ROASTED ROCK

Where exposed on hillsides or gullies, coal seams are sometimes ignited by forest and grass fires, lightning, or even by spontaneous combustion. Once started, fires spread inward along the seam. As coal is burned and reduced to ash, support is lost and overlying material cracks and collapses. These fissures feed oxygen to the fire. Burning continues until the fire burns back to a point where the overlying strata are so thick that cracks no longer reach to the surface. Deprived of its oxygen supply, the fire is smothered.

Clinker, sometimes incorrectly referred to as scoria, is the baked red sandstone and shale that lie above a burned coal steam. These are literally "cooked" rocks. Heated to high temperatures, oxygen combined with iron in the rock to form iron oxide, producing the bands of red rust color so prevalent on hillsides in many areas of southeast Montana.

The heat responsible for the coloration also hardens the rocks, and when hit together they make an obvious "clinking" sound — thus the name. Clinker is one of the best road surfacing materials and explains the red color of some highways in coal country. It is also used for landscaping both in and out of the region.

INTERNAL DRAINAGE

Not all of Great Plains Montana drains to the Missouri or Yellowstone rivers. Surface waters within a 600-square-mile basin between the Musselshell and Yellowstone drain internally and don't contribute a drop of surface runoff to outside waterways. Approximately 40 miles long and 15 miles wide, this distinctive area extends from Acton on the east to beyond Broadview on the north, south to Molt, and west past Rapelje.

The basin actually consists of two component basins, Lake Basin on the west and Comanche Basin to the east. Intermittent streams within these drainages merely carry their flows toward central low sections where they form lakes. Some are seasonal and are present only during periods of heavy runoff. Hailstone Lake and nearby Big Lake within the Lake Basin are larger and more nearly permanent than others. But even their shorelines are marked by bands of white salt deposits, more reminiscent of Nevada than Montana, left by evaporation and fluctuating lake size. Hailstone Lake is part of the national wildlife refuge of the same name, but its 660 acres isn't home to a single fish owing to its shallow and salty nature.

Prairie
Mountains and Highlands

For some, Eastern Montana is at its scenic best in the northwestern corner where island-like mountains and highlands add visual variety to the landscape. Here forest-clad sentinels rise above surrounding plains adding interest to one of the most unique sections anywhere in the North American plains. South Dakota has its Black Hills, and Wyoming its Devil's Tower, but nowhere else in the Great Plains is there such a mountain-studded landscape. To residents of the area the names are familiar — the Little Rockies, Highwoods, Bear Paws, Big and Little Snowies, Judiths, Moccasins, Sweetgrass Hills and more. Often referred to as Rocky Mountain outliers, their evolution is linked to the same forces which produced the main range to the west.

> South Dakota has its Black Hills, and Wyoming its Devil's Tower, but nowhere else in the Great Plains is there such a mountain-studded landscape.

Recent dating of associated rocks suggests that beginning between 60 and 70 million years ago molten material from great depth was forced upward toward the surface in the areas that now constitute the Judith, Moccasin and Little Rocky mountains. This flood of viscous magma worked its way up through layers of sandstone and shale and other sedimentary rocks, but did not reach the surface. Instead, at varying depths, it spread laterally between adjacent layers of rocks

before solidifying. These irregular to circular shaped intrusives, called laccoliths, were blister shaped and usually less than a few miles across.

Today these hard igneous rocks are exposed in each of the three mountain ranges. Since their emplacement, a continual regional uplift, linked to the ongoing evolution of the Rockies, accelerated erosion and stripped away more easily eroded overlying sedimentary rocks. Because of their resistant nature, they now stand out as highlands.

Each of the higher peaks in the Judith Mountains is an unearthed laccolith. Granitic Judith Peak at 6,428 feet is the highest, but others also exceed 6,000 feet. Names such as Crystal Peak, Porphyry Peak, and Gold Hill are indicative of the mineralization associated with these laccolith formations. The Judith Mountains are peppered with abandoned mines like the New Year, Spotted Horse, Whiskey Gulch and Old Glory. Mineral production was sufficient in at least two areas to justify the development of Giltedge and Maiden, both now ghost towns.

11

Rather than a single range, the Moccasin Mountains, just west of the Judiths, are actually two detached highlands, the North Moccasins and the South Moccasins. South Peak, at 5,420 feet, is near the center of the southern intrusive body. North of Warm Spring Creek the highest peak in the North Moccasins rises to 5,581 feet. The early 20th century ghost town of Kendall and other abandoned mines in the North Moccasins are evidence of mineralization in that area.

An interesting feature on the southern flank of the North Moccasins is a two-square-mile terrace, or bench, of flat land. This step-like feature is built of gravel that eroded from higher areas to the north. Known locally as The Park its flat nature and grass cover contrast with the encircling sloping and forested land.

For the Indians, the Little Rockies were sacred, for Kid Curry and other outlaws its canyons meant safe refuge, and for thousands of miners, its gold was their hoped-for ticket to wealth.

To the northeast, just beyond the Missouri, are the Little Rocky Mountains, perhaps the most island-like of Montana's mountain outliers. Rising more than two thousand feet above the surrounding plains, the Little Rockies have intrigued and lured man for centuries. For Indians the mountains were sacred, for Kid Curry and other outlaws its canyons meant safe refuge, and for thousands of miners, its gold was their hoped-for ticket to wealth. Like the Judiths and Moccasins, the core of this highland is made up of igneous intrusives formed when molten rock squeezed between other rock layers and fissures. Sedimentary rocks have been eroded from the central portion, exposing the now dormant laccoliths.

Around the flanks of the highlands are upturned layers of older sedimentary rocks, which had been pierced and pushed upward by the intrusion some 60 million years ago. These now form a concentric, irregular bull's-eye pattern around the central igneous mass. Some stand up as virtual walls 600 to 700 feet tall. Numerous caves have developed in the upturned limestone rocks on the south flank of the mountains.

Old Scraggy is the highest peak in the Little Rockies at 5,708 feet, although a half dozen others approach or exceed 5,500 feet, including appropriately named Gold Bug Butte, at 5,450 feet. Not the highest, but clearly the most noteworthy, is Eagle Child Mountain in the western portion of the range, south of Hays. This was revered as the most sacred mountain to the Gros Ventre Indians. Young braves and medicine men seeking spiritual power made pilgrimages to the 5,243-foot summit for vision quests. They were to remain for four days and four nights while they fasted and communed with the spirits. According to local legend, most were frightened off the mountain by bloodcurdling visions of giant serpents and enormous animals before the fourth night!

Above: *Moccasin Mountains near Stanford.* — Rick Graetz

Below: *Little Rocky Mountains from the Missouri breaks.* — Rick Graetz

Above: *The Sweetgrass Hills.* — Rick Graetz

Below: *Bearpaw Mountains, end of Chief Joseph's 2,000 mile Nez Perce retreat of 1877.* — Rick Graetz

Reaching 2,500 feet above the plains, the Sweetgrass Hills are visible for a hundred miles on a clear day.

Following a several-million-year period of relative quiet, northcentral Montana experienced a new episode of igneous activity. This time, molten material not only reached near the surface, it flowed out as lava and, in some places, spewed from volcanoes.

Beginning about 50 million years ago, laccoliths intruded in a 25-mile-long arc under the area of the present-day Sweetgrass Hills. Most of these intrusives clustered in three groupings corresponding with today's West, Middle and East Buttes. West Butte at 6,981 feet is the highest in the Hills, but the East Butte has several peaks above 6,000 feet. South of the main Sweetgrass Hills, Grassy and Haystack buttes, two other exposed laccoliths, rise as lone sentinels 700 to 800 feet above the surrounding plains.

Reaching 2,500 feet above the plains, the Sweetgrass Hills are visible for a hundred miles on a clear day, and were an important landmark for the migrating Blackfeet Indians. Presence of tipi rings today suggests they used the slopes of these forested highlands as seasonal hunting camps. Later, in the 1890s, gold-bearing deposits in the Middle Butte attracted hundreds of miners. The little-known town of Gold Butte, which developed south of the mines to serve the local population, was short-lived.

Twenty-five miles south of Havre the peaks of the Bear Paw Mountains punctuate the landscape. They contain the largest area and volume of igneous rocks in northcentral Montana. Geologically, their origin is more complex than many of Montana's outliers. Trending east-west through the central portion of the mountains is an anticline, a broad upwarp in the underlying strata. It was bowed upward during the formation of the Rocky Mountains. Piercing these now exposed sedimentary rocks are numerous laccoliths and other associated intrusives.

Igneous rocks of the central Bear Paw Mountain Arch solidified underground, but rocks to the north and south are extrusives. They spewed onto the surface as molten lava and today form two large volcanic fields geologically more reminiscent of Yellowstone National Park than most other areas in Eastern Montana. The southern field covers approximately 300 square miles and the northern only slightly less. In places this veneer of volcanic material is itself pierced by intrusive igneous rock.

Geologists now assume that some of these intrusives are merely the remnants of subsurface plumbing that fed active volcanoes some 50 million years ago. They would have been merely the conduits through which lava flowed to the surface. Millions of years of erosion have erased the outline of long-extinct volcanoes, and today we are left with wide valley areas between fairly low, rounded crests. Still, the mountains rise high enough to justify Eastern Montana's only commercial ski area.

To the resident Blackfeet of the 18th and 19th centuries, this landscape evidently suggested the outline of a bear's claw, since that was their name for the mountains. For Chief Joseph and the Nez Perce, Snake Creek on the northeast flank of the mountains marked the end of their infamous 1877 retreat. After traveling almost 2,000 miles and coming within 39 miles of their Canadian destination, the chief and his party were captured by Colonel Nelson Miles.

13

The Highwood Mountains probably hold the most interest of all of Montana's outlying mountains for the amateur geologist and mineral collector.

For the amateur geologist and mineral collector, the Highwood Mountains probably hold the greatest interest of all Montana outliers. Located 30 miles east of Great Falls, they resemble, geologically, the Bear Paws still further east. They, too, are a group of 50-million-year-old extinct volcanoes long since deeply eroded. As in the Bear Paws, there is an associated volcanic field, this one approximately 120 square miles in size. Highwood Peak is the tallest in the range. It rises to 7,625 feet in the center of the volcanic field and may be the remnant of the region's biggest volcano.

Intrusive rocks, those that solidified before reaching the surface, are also exposed in the area. Included are laccoliths like those in many neighboring outliers. Square Butte, ten miles east of the Highwoods, is one of these exhumed laccoliths. Although only 5,680 feet high, it rises 2,400 feet above the surrounding plains and is a regional landmark. Ringed by cliffs, its 2,000-acre flat top is a majestic platform from which to view the surrounding countryside. Designation of the butte by the Bureau of Land Management as a Natural Area should help assure the protection of this unique feature.

Dikes are another eye-catching intrusive found on the flanks of the highlands. These are wall-like intrusions of igneous rocks which squeezed their way up through vertical fissures in the overlying sedimentary rocks and cooled before reaching the surface. Stripped of their surrounding sandstone or limestone, these more resistant rocks are left as narrow ridges which radiate outward like spokes of a wheel. The dikes and laccoliths of the Highwoods have yielded some of the world's best sapphire and are known by mineralogists and gem collectors the world over.

Tucked up against the Rockies southwest of Great Falls is yet another, even older, forested highland of volcanic origin. Most Montanans would probably have difficulty naming this 300-square-mile elevated tract — the Adel Mountains. Driving Interstate 15 between Craig and Cascade, one passes through the center of this pile of volcanic material that flowed over the area some 70 million years ago. One peak reaches just over 7,000 feet, but most are significantly lower. Few recreationists seek out these mountains, but those who do are rewarded with fascinating geological features. Weathered volcanic rocks have been eroded into intriguing landscapes such as the Devil's Kitchen, The Pinnacles, and The Sawteeth.

Montanans probably are more familiar with the swarm of laccoliths just north of the Adels. Here, in the apex between the Sun and Missouri rivers, a cluster of more than a half dozen intrusives rises from the plains. Among them are Cascade Butte, Haystack Butte, Crown Butte and Shaw Butte, each a landmark. The area moved Charles Russell, Montana's noted western artist, who chose it as a setting for many of his Old West paintings. Flat-topped and symmetrical Square Butte, seven miles south of Fort Shaw, is recognizable in the background of several of Russell's works. For him, the landscape captured the mood of an earlier era when range riders or Blackfeet in battle array might be seen on the horizon.

The area between the Sun and Missouri contains half a dozen buttes — each a landmark. They moved Charles Russell, who chose this setting for many of his Old West paintings.

Left: *Round Butte from Square Butte, Highwood Mountains in background.* — Jim Romo

Right: *Shaw Butte.* — John Alwin

15

South and east of the Judiths, several other prairie mountains and highlands project above the Eastern Montana plains. Geologically, they are distinct from most of the northcentral Montana outliers. One class includes the Big and Little Snowy mountains, Pryors and Bighorns. Each corresponds with a broad arch-like uplift in the ancient underlying rocks of the earth's crust, warped upward during the formation of the main spine of the Rockies.

Continued uplift and erosion have opened window-like holes in the overlying sediment to expose the ancient 600-million-plus-year-old rocks in the core of the Big Snowy Mountains. Most of the rocks exposed in the range are sedimentary layers uplifted when the crust rose about 60 or 70 million years ago. We see them today, draped over the mountain's core. Their homogeneous and gently sloping nature are reflected in the Snowies' relatively smooth outline. Although the Big Snowies rise to impressive heights, the crest of the range is rather tame, lacking the large-scale relief associated with outliers further north.

Forests cover much of both the Big and Little Snowies, and extensive areas are within the Lewis and Clark National Forest. For the residents of nearby Lewistown and surrounding central Montana plains, the Snowies are an outdoor playground. Crystal Lake, nestled below 8,800-foot peaks in the western part of the range, is a popular destination.

Except for the gravel road which penetrates into the Crystal Lake area, the Big Snowies remain roadless. The area provides an excellent retreat for those seeking solitude and wilderness recreation. Most of the range is now being considered for inclusion in the national wilderness system.

Like the Snowies, both the Pryor Mountains and the Big Horn Mountains correspond with areas where the earth's crust and overlying strata have been bowed upward. As we mentioned in defining Eastern Montana, both ranges should be thought of as part of the Middle Rocky Mountain Province. They have been included here since most Montanans consider them and the surrounding area to be a part of Eastern Montana.

The Pryors' numerous ice caves and 32,000-acre, wild-horse range attract thousands of visitors annually.

West of the Bighorn River the Pryors rise to a maximum elevation of 8,800 feet, but, as with the Snowies, mountain tops are relatively level. Relief is most pronounced along the faulted east flank of both Big Pryor and East Pryor mountains. Stream erosion has incised deep canyons and dissected the flanks of the plateau-like masses of 300-million-year-old limestone. A large swath in the central portion of the range is part of Custer National Forest. Its southeast corner is now under consideration for wilderness status. The Pryors' numerous ice caves and 32,000-acre wild-horse range attract thousands of visitors annually.

East of the impressive Bighorn Canyon and Bighorn Lake, the northern end of the bold Bighorn Mountains reaches across the Montana border out of Wyoming. The range consists of an uplifted core of ancient granite. Within the central portion of the range in Wyoming this granite is exposed and rises to more than 13,000 feet. But in the Montana portion a sedimentary veneer covers the underlying core, and in only one small area have sediments been stripped away to expose granite. Here, uplands reach a nearly uniform elevation of around 8,500 feet before dropping to the level of the adjacent plains.

Differential erosion of sedimentary rocks, not upwarped crustal material, volcanoes and laccoliths, explain the remaining major prairie highlands. The largest of these in area are the Bull Mountains south of Roundup, known as the Bull's Nose to the Blackfeet. Better described as prominent forest-covered hills than mountains, they correspond with an area of resistant Tertiary sandstone that has withstood erosion better than older surrounding sedimentary rocks. An erosional remnant, the region now stands in relief that reaches up to 1,800 feet above the surrounding plains. Heavily dissected by stream erosion, the mountains lack a central spine and form an irregular maze of resistant sandstone ridges. Interbedded layers of coal, some of which is mined, is related geologically to coal in the Colstrip-Decker area.

The north-south trending Wolf, or Rosebud, Mountains just east of the Little Bighorn River correspond with the exposed edge of a gently inclined sandstone layer that protrudes above the surface. More resistant than surrounding rocks, it stands up in relief, forming a cuesta, which is an elevation of land with gentle slopes on one side and cliffs on the other. This broken ridge extends for a distance of about 40 miles, with highest peaks reaching elevations just over 5,000 feet.

Differential erosion again helps explain the presence of the Big Sheep and Little Sheep Mountains northwest of Terry. Rather than a resistant layer of sandstone, these shale deposits are capped by up to 30 feet of gravel. More hills than mountains, the highest point is only 3,500 to 3,600 feet in elevation.

Major island-like mountains and highlands add landscape variety to Great Plains Montana, but they account for a small percentage of the area. Much more typical are smaller, lower, and often isolated buttes and knolls which do not merit a mountain label. Like the Rosebud-Wolf Mountains or Big Sheep Mountains, they, too, usually owe their existence to their resistant sandstone or a present or recent capping of other strong material.

Left: *The Pryor Mountains guard the Bighorn Canyon on the west.* — Rick Graetz

Above: *The Big Snowy Mountains and,* **Right,** *its popular Crystal Lake.* — Mark Thompson

Below: *The Little Sheep mountains north of Terry.* — Emanual Schlabach

These erosional remnants are too numerous to mention individually, but their variety can be illustrated with some well-known examples. The resistance of sandstone layers to erosion is evident to Billings residents every day in the dramatic Rimrocks which rise like a wall from the Yellowstone River Valley. This buff-colored layer is the Cretaceous Eagle Sandstone. Only 36 miles downstream, Pompey's Pillar stands as an erosional remnant of a somewhat younger sandstone unit. The towering 200-foot-high sentinel adjacent to the river caught Captain William Clark's attention when he passed by in 1806. He named the pillar after Sacajawea's infant and carved his signature and the date in the rock. The monolith has been designated a National Historic Landmark and today's visitors are still able to read his 170-year-old autograph.

The towering 200-foot-high sentinel adjacent to the river caught Captain William Clark's attention when he passed by in 1806 and named it Pompey's Pillar.

Twelve miles north of Ekalaka, in 220-acre Medicine Rocks State Park, resistant sandstone rocks rise above the prairie in weird and contorted shapes. Angular formations stand out as pyramids, spires, pinnacles, arches and other shapes, sculpted by water and wind erosion. Indians conducted their ceremonials in the mystic atmosphere of these oddly eroded shapes. Southwest of Ekalaka are Montana's picturesque Chalk Buttes. These are Tertiary age sediments that include siltstone, sandstone and associated volcanic ash and stream deposited volcanic material. Weathering has changed some of the ash to clays. It is these clays, especially bentonite, that give the Buttes their white color, not chalk as the name suggests. Crowning resistant sandstone layers have protected these underlying sediments from erosion, and they remain one of Montana's most unique geological formations.

Top: *Pompey's Pillar downstream from Billings. Captain Clark's name still can be read where he inscribed it in 1806.* — Rick Graetz

Middle: *The Medicine Rocks and,* **Below,** *the Chalk Buttes dot the landscape of far southeastern Montana.* — Rick Graetz

The horizontal dimension dominates in much of Eastern Montana — especially in areas covered by continental glaciation. — Rick Graetz

ICE LEAVES ITS MARK

Try picturing this: the site of the city of Great Falls without the Missouri River, or sitting at the bottom of a lake 600 feet deep. How about the Missouri flowing down the valley of what is now home to the Milk River. Far-fetched as they sound, these probably would have been accurate descriptions of Montana geography in the not-too-distant past. To understand these and some other present-day surface features in the northern section of Eastern Montana, we have to return to the time of the last Ice Age.

> Picture this: the site of the city of Great Falls without the Missouri River, or sitting at the bottom of a lake 600 feet deep.

Between about 10,000 and 140,000 years ago, only yesterday in geologic time, sections of Eastern Montana north of the Missouri were twice covered by large glaciers hundreds of feet thick. These were merely the southern fringe of gigantic continental glaciers that spread outward from an ice cap in the Hudson Bay area of northern Canada, covering much of that country and reaching into the United States as far south as Iowa. Even at the southern limit in Montana the glaciers had enough power to literally rearrange some aspects of our state's physical geography.

Evidence of the ice and its influx are abundant, although all the details have not yet been deciphered. Still, based on work done by geologists in the early 1900s, it is possible to sketch some of the chapters in this fascinating story.

As the ice sheets spread southward through Canada, they scraped up and pushed along debris. Some of this material found its way to Montana. Today, for example, scattered across the plains north of the Missouri are thousands of large rocks and boulders that were carried into the state and then were deposited when the ice melted. Sometimes these glacial erratics are as large as a car. To geologists, these are especially valuable for determining the glaciers' direction of movement since it is sometimes possible to link erratics with their area of origin. Rock types of some erratics tell us they were transplanted from northern Saskatchewan and northern Manitoba, distances of more than 500 miles.

The former maximum thickness of an ice sheet in an area sometimes can be estimated from the maximum elevation of erratics and other glacial deposits. In the northern Montana plains, we have to look to the prairie mountains and highlands for evidence. Northwest of the Bear Paws and four miles east of Box Elder, 3,650-foot Square Butte rises almost 1,000 feet above the plains. The presence of glacially derived granite boulders atop this landmark suggests that the ice was thick enough to move over its top. This would mean a thickness of at least 1,000 feet!

Only the highest outliers in the path of the ice escaped being covered. The Highwoods, Bear Paws and Little Rockies were large and high enough to thwart the southward movement in those areas. Ice lapped up along their northern flanks, and in the case of the Bear Paws was deflected around the sides. Field evidence is inconclusive, but the tops of the Sweetgrass Hills probably were high enough to protrude above the ice, three islands in a frozen sea.

These glaciated plains of northern Montana include some of the flattest and most muted terrain in the state. Overriding ice not only scoured down and rounded high points, glacial material it left behind filled lower areas and contributed to an overall softening of the natural landscape. As the last vestige of ice melted and retreated northward across the border about 10,000 years ago, it left behind a more subdued and flatter landscape. Today's grain farmers of northeastern Montana and the Golden Triangle area can thank this past glacial action for its contribution to the flat to gently rolling land that is a prerequisite to their extensive and mechanized farming.

> The grain farmers of northeastern Montana and the Golden Triangle can thank this past glacial action for its contribution to the flat to gently rolling land that is a prerequisite to their extensive mechanized farming.

The earliest of what may have been Eastern Montana's two ice ages dates from approximately 70,000 to 140,000 years ago. It was the most extensive, and evidence suggests it was powerful enough to literally change the course of the Missouri River.

In preglacial time the Missouri probably veered in an easterly direction south of Great Falls, by-passing that city site, and flowing from west to east through what is now Sand Coulee. Today tiny, intermittent Sand Coulee Creek looks out of place as it flows east to west through its oversized valley.

Judging from its meandering nature, and because its cross-section is similar to nearby stretches of the Missouri, chances are this valley that carries Sand Coulee Creek once carried the mighty Missouri. At the time, the river continued eastward, eventually swinging northward to join its present course near the mouth of Belt

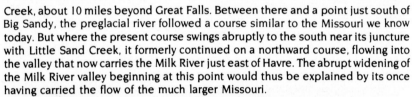

Creek, about 10 miles beyond Great Falls. Between there and a point just south of Big Sandy, the preglacial river followed a course similar to the Missouri we know today. But where the present course swings abruptly to the south near its juncture with Little Sand Creek, it formerly continued on a northward course, flowing into the valley that now carries the Milk River just east of Havre. The abrupt widening of the Milk River valley beginning at this point would thus be explained by its once having carried the flow of the much larger Missouri.

Glacial Lake Great Falls grew to cover approximately 1,200 square miles, seven times the size of Flathead Lake.

The advance of the oldest ice sheet into Northern Montana deranged this drainage pattern. At the time of its maximum extent a tongue of ice reached the Sand Coulee area where it formed an ice dam, holding back the flow of the Missouri. Water backed up, eventually forming Glacial Lake Great Falls. The lake grew to cover approximately 1,200 square miles, seven times the size of Flathead Lake. It submerged an area roughly bounded by Choteau, Cascade, Belt and Dutton. If present today, it would be the country's largest natural freshwater lake west of the Great Lakes. Located near the lake's eastern shore, the site of Great Falls lay submerged under 600 feet of water!

Blocked by a wall of ice to the north, the lake sought a new outlet. A spectacular spillway developed along the northern flank of the Highwood Mountains, just south of the ice sheet. Vast quantities of water flowing through the area eroded a deep valley up to a mile wide and 500 feet deep, now known as the Shonkin Sag. Beyond the sag Missouri waters flowed through a new channel which passed south of the Bear Paw and Little Rocky mountains before joining its former preglacial course near Fort Peck.

Melting and retreat of the glacier from the Great Falls area to north of Fort Benton allowed Missouri waters to begin cutting a new and lower spillway. It was at this time that the river's course between Great Falls and the mouth of Arrow Creek, 120 miles downriver, shifted northward and began eroding its present course.

Above Left: *The town of Shonkin occupies a former channel of the Missouri River as did Dry Falls,* **Above,** *northeast of The Highwood Mountains.* — John Alwin, Ken Turner

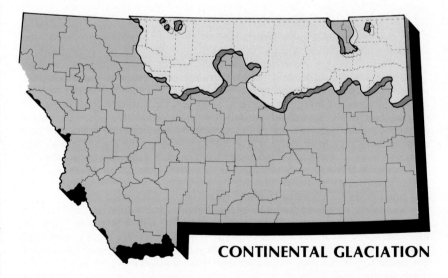

CONTINENTAL GLACIATION

Extent of Continental glaciation in Eastern Montana — *U.S. Geological Survey.*

WATERS WITHIN

On the semiarid plains of Montana water is an especially critical and valuable resource. Fortunately, the region is adjacent to well watered highlands on the west and southwest which serve as headwater areas for all major Eastern Montana rivers. Highlands contribute most of the flow to the area's crucial rivers, enough to carry them across the dry plains where little flow is added. To Eastern Montanans their names have a familiar ring: among them, the Missouri and Yellowstone, Sun, Teton, Marias, Milk, Bighorn, Tongue and Powder. Indians once camped on their shores and later, initial white settlement was funneled along their courses. Today they supply essential waters for farmers and ranchers, municipalities, industries, hydropower generation, recreationists and still support abundant and varied flora and fauna. Without these life-giving waters, Eastern Montana would be a very different place.

Great Plains Montana is part of the expansive Missouri River Basin which drains to the Gulf of Mexico via the Mississippi. A small wedge-shaped mountainous area just east of the Continental Divide in northeastern Glacier National Park and extending a few miles east out of the park drains via St. Mary River to Hudson Bay, and although east of the Divide, is not within the Great Plains. Waters within Eastern Montana are collected in two main river systems — the Missouri and the Yellowstone. The Missouri drainage is the largest, covering approximately the northern two-thirds of Great Plains Montana. The Yellowstone and its tributaries drain the remainder of the Montana plains.

> The mighty Missouri actually ranks fourth in average annual flow, after western Montana's Clark Fork and Kootenai rivers, and even lower than its major tributary, the Yellowstone.

Ask Montanans which one of their rivers carries the greatest volume of water as it flows out of the state and the majority would probably respond, "The Missouri, of course." Long-term records show otherwise. The mighty Missouri actually ranks fourth, after western Montana's Clark Fork and Kootenai rivers, and even lower than its major tributary, the Yellowstone. The 10,000-cubic-feet-per-second average annual flow at Culbertson is less than half the figure for the Clark Fork as it crosses the Idaho state line. Although not the largest, the Missouri may well be Montana's most historic waterway. Few would argue that it remains the state's most prized renewable water resource.

The Missouri River north of Fort Benton. — Len Eckel

The Missouri begins at the Three Forks with the combined waters of the Jefferson, Madison and Gallatin rivers. All but a tiny portion of their flows originates within southwestern Montana's broad valley Rockies. Well watered highlands including the Gallatin, Madison, Gravelly, Pioneer and Tobacco Root all contribute to these Missouri tributaries.

The Missouri and its tributaries have profoundly seasonal flows. But unlike the Yellowstone drainage, where major flow-control structures are minimal, a multitude of dams and reservoirs alter flows within the Missouri basin. Reservoirs range from headwater impoundments like alpine Hyalite south of Bozeman to the sequence of much larger reservoirs in Canyon Ferry, Hauser and Holter on the mainstream of the Missouri north of Townsend.

Although upstream from our Eastern Montana region, these dams and reservoirs do affect the Missouri downriver. Each holds back peak spring flows to be released during other seasons. Canyon Ferry alone has the capacity to retain 2,051,000 acre-feet of water — enough to cover 2,051,000 acres under one foot of water! Irrigation is a primary purpose for the existence of most of these reservoirs, but some are truly multipurpose. Canyon Ferry not only serves irrigators, it is also designated a flood-control dam; has associated fish, wildlife and recreational functions; and generates electricity as its waters flow through the turbines at Canyon Ferry Dam.

After passing through the stair-stepped sequence of large artificial lakes east of Helena, the Missouri picks up the waters of a right-bank tributary, the Dearborn, and then snakes through its narrow gorge bisecting the Adel Mountains, and finally enters Great Plains Montana. Here the grain of the natural landscape changes, and so, too, does the river. Issuing from the mountains the river enters the Chestnut Valley and the level floor of former Glacial Lake Great Falls. For its initial 300 miles the river is confined and diverted by mountainous terrain, but between the Adels and Great Falls the lazy river meanders freely over its broad flood plain, falling a mere 85 feet in a distance of 75 miles. Crescent-shaped oxbow lakes fringe its path and provide clues to the river's former course.

> Between the Adels and Great Falls the lazy river meanders over its broad flood plain, falling a mere 85 feet in a distance of 75 miles.

At the city of Great Falls, the river's personality again changes. Beyond the confluence of the Sun the Missouri enters a narrow canyon with sheer cliffs of shale and sandstone. Over the course of the next dozen miles it drops more than 600 feet in elevation. In places along this reach, interbedded iron-rich layers in the underlying sandstone rock resisted erosion and produced a sequence of spectacular rapids and cascades.

Plains Indians knew well of these falls and were no less in awe of their beauty and power than Captain Meriwether Lewis when he became the first white man to visit and describe them in 1805. Ascending the river Lewis was attracted by the distant roar of falling water and the sight of spray rising from the plains "like a column of smoke." Proceeding he came upon the legendary Great Falls the Indians had mentioned. He sat opposite the falls and recorded the first written description of this "sublimely grand spectacle," thereby providing a priceless legacy. His account remains one of the most eloquent ever written of this thundering 75-foot cascade. Further upstream Lewis discovered numerous rapids and cascades including additional large falls ranging up to a 37-foot-tall cataract he left unnamed, but eventually became known as Rainbow Falls.

MERIWETHER LEWIS DESCRIBES THE GREAT FALLS

On June 13, 1805, Captain Meriwether Lewis became the first white man of record to view the Great Falls of the Missouri. His first impressions, recorded in his journal, read as follows:

Immediately at the cascade the river is about 300 yards wide, about 90 or 100 yards of which, next the larboard bluff, is a smooth sheet of water, falling over a precipice of at least eighty feet; the remaining part about 200 yards on my right forms the grandest sight I ever beheld; the height of the fall is the same as the other part but the irregular and somewhat projecting rocks below receive the water in its passage down and break it into a perfect white foam which assumes a thousand forms in a moment; sometimes flying up in jets of sparkling foam to the height of fifteen or twenty feet and are scarcely formed until large bodies of the same beaten and foaming water are thrown over and conceal them. In short, the rocks seem to be most happily fixed to present a sheet of the whitest beaten froth for 200 yards in length and eight feet perpendicular.

Rainbow Dam near Great Falls. — C. L. McGee

Above: *Marias River north of Valier.* — Rick Graetz

Below: *La Barge Rock on the Missouri.* — Jim Romo

Today, these great falls are harnessed. Any river with a generous flow and high falls constitutes one of the most desirable hydroelectric landscapes. To hydraulic engineers the combination is seen as "head" and means potential power. Massive run-of-river hydroelectric dams, including Ryan Dam at the Great Falls, now capture this clean power which is distributed throughout Eastern Montana.

Beyond the harnessed stretch, the Missouri enters a wider valley which carries it northeastward. Past historic Fort Benton, long the head of steamship navigation on the Missouri, the river moves toward its confluence with the Marias, named by Meriwether Lewis for his cousin, Maria Wood. The Lewis and Clark expedition confused this river with the mainstream of the Missouri and was delayed for more than a week. Such confusion suggests that well-above-average snowmelt and/or spring rains must have swelled the Marias that June of 1805. This tributary usually carries less than a third of the Missouri's volume at their juncture, and under average conditions it is obvious that the Marias is the tributary.

The Marias, its Teton tributary and other right-bank Missouri tributaries like the Sun drain the Rockies' east slope and have peak June flows, but usually markedly lower flows than those of the record 1964 flood. Numerous reservoirs reservoirs hold back some of these peak flows. Lake Elwell behind Tiber Dam on the Marias is the third largest reservoir in Montana's Missouri Basin.

THE 1964 FLOOD

The potential for well-above-average June flows on the Marias and other rivers draining the east slopes of the Rockies startled residents of northwestern Great Plains Montana in early June of 1964. During a 30-hour storm on the 7th and 8th of the month, record precipitation totals of up to 14 inches coupled with melting of a lingering mountain snowpack swelled streams. Dams overflowed, and in some cases were destroyed, towns such as Augusta and Choteau were flooded, 30 people lost their lives, and damage totaled more than $50 million.

Dams may block these rivers and their headwater drainages, but the Missouri itself remains free flowing for the 149 miles between Fort Benton and the Fred Robinson Bridge. Federal designation in 1976 of this section as the Upper Missouri Wild and Scenic River should assure continued protection for this primitive and priceless remnant of an untamed Missouri.

The undammed reach of the Missouri is considered an easy and enjoyable section to float. Rapids are minimal and the generally slow moving waters carry floaters along at a leisurely pace of four to five miles per hour. The trip downstream from Fort Benton to U.S. Highway 191 provides scenic vistas that remain as described in the journals of the Lewis and Clark expedition. One must float this stretch to truly experience its beauty. The Bureau of Land Management's map pair of the reach, available at their Lewistown offices, is recommended for all floaters.

A 1978 amending act to the 1976 legislation instructed the Secretary of the Interior to determine "which of the three classes — wild river, scenic river, or recreation river — best fit portions of the river segment, designate such portions in such classes, and prepare a management plan for the river area in accordance with such designation." The Upper Missouri Wild and Scenic River is now managed in seven segments — three wild reaches essentially unchanged by man totaling 64 miles; two scenic, largely wild, without impoundments but having occasional road access, for a combined length of 26 miles; and two recreational segments readily accessible by road equaling 59 miles.

> The most distinctive rock formations are found on the White Rocks segment between Coal Banks Landing and Slaughter River Campsite. Here, along a 40-mile section, towering white cliffs fire the imagination, yielding landmarks like Fortress Rock, LaBarge Rock, Eagle Rock, Citadel Rock, Hole-In-The-Wall and Steamboat Rock.

Today's visitors are treated to a kaleidoscope of natural beauty. Banks are built of generally flat lying sedimentary strata that are literally layers of time. These are the sandstones, shales and coal deposits laid in sequence beginning 80 million years ago when this area was beneath a huge inland sea. In places, intrusions of younger, dark igneous rocks crosscut these sedimentary units.

The most distinctive rock formations are found on the White Rocks segment between Coal Banks Landing and Slaughter River Campsite. Here, along a 40-mile section, towering white cliffs of the Eagle Sandstone, the same formation that forms Billings Rimrocks, reach skyward. Erosion and other geologic activity have produced extraordinary rock formations that fired Captain Lewis' imagination in the spring of 1805 and continue to amaze river travelers. Fortress Rock, LaBarge Rock, Eagle Rock, Citadel Rock, Hole-in-the-Wall and Steamboat Rock are some of the most notable of these architectural-like landmarks. These and hundreds of other honeycombed and pedestaled rocks, monuments, spires, windows, arches and vertical, igneous rock walls beckon passersby to let their imaginations run free.

Above: *Hole-in-the-Wall on the Missouri River.* — Len Eckel

Below: *White Rocks area, Missouri River.* — Rick Graetz

MERIWETHER LEWIS AT THE WHITE CLIFFS

Viewing the Missouri's "White Cliffs" area on May 31, 1805, Meriwether Lewis wrote:

The hills and river clifts which we passed today exhibit a most romantic appearance. The bluffs of the river rise to the height of from 2 to 300 feet and in most places nearly perpendicular; they are formed of remarkable white sandstone which is sufficiently soft to give way readily to the impression of water; two or three thin horizontal stratas of white freestone, on which the rains or water made no impression, lie imbeded in these clifts of soft stone near the upper part of them; . . . The water in the course of time in decending from these hills and plains on either side of the river has trickled down the soft sand clifts and woarn it into a thousand grotesque figures, which with the help of a little imagination and an oblique view, at a distance are made to represent eligant ranges of lofty freestone buildings, having their parapets well stocked with statuary; collumns of various sculpture both grooved and plain, are also seen supporting long galleries in front of those buildings.

24

In addition to its scenic beauty, the upper Missouri is also an irreplaceable legacy of the historic American West. Evidence of its place in history is legion along this 149-mile reach. All 11 campsites used by the epic Lewis and Clark expedition between May 24 and June 11, 1805 have been located and identified. Today's visitors can climb to the spot near Cow Island Landing where Captain Lewis first thought he saw the Rocky Mountains.

Scattered graves, sandstone dugouts and rotting woodpiles are ghostly reminders of the small army of woodhawks who supplied the necessary fuel to this growing flotilla of shallow-draft, paddle-wheeled craft.

From the time of Lewis and Clark to the arrival of railroads in the 1880s, the Missouri was the transportation corridor to the northern Rocky Mountain-Great Plains area. Fur trappers and traders were the first white men to use this water passage pioneered by Lewis and Clark. Soon, their keelboats, Mackinaws, bull boats and canoes routinely plied these waters, which provided direct linkage between the fur-rich upper Missouri and the St. Louis market downstream on the Mississippi. The sites of their former trading posts of Fort McKenzie, Fort Chardon and Fort Lewis lie within the wild and scenic section.

Here too, at the mouth of the Judith, was the short-lived military post of Camp Cooke, defending river traffic from Indian raids during the late 1860s. Nearby, in 1846, the famous Catholic missionary, Father DeSmet, met with the Flathead and Blackfeet, and nine years later Washington Territorial Governor Isaac Stevens presided over a large treaty council.

When the mode of river traffic shifted to steamboats in the 1860s most fur trade posts already had faded. Only one made the successful transition from fur post to town — Fort Benton. Its location at the head of steamship navigation helped assure its success as a distribution center, and it boomed in unison with the gold discoveries of western Montana. Scattered graves, sandstone dugouts and rotting woodpiles are ghostly reminders of the small army of woodhawks who supplied the necessary fuel to this growing flotilla of shallow-draft, paddle-wheeled craft. The arrival of railroads in the 1880s effectively ended this colorful era of waterborne commerce.

Lewis and Clark passing down the Missouri today below the Wild and Scenic Rivers portion would scarcely recognize the waterway. Gone is 135 miles of the river and in its place is gigantic Fort Peck Reservoir. With an area of almost 400 square miles and a 1,600-mile shoreline, the lake now submerges the former river's course under as much as 200 feet of water. When full, the reservoir holds enough water to flood, to a depth of one foot, an area larger than Vermont, New Hampshire and Massachusetts combined.

When full, Fort Peck Reservoir holds enough water to flood, to a depth of one foot, an area larger than Vermont, New Hampshire, and Massachusetts combined.

Equally as grand as the reservoir is massive Fort Peck Dam which holds it. With a length of 21,000 feet, it is one of the world's largest earth-filled dams.

Abandoned homestead in the Missouri breaks. — Jim Romo

The Fort Peck complex began in 1933 as a Public Works project under the Roosevelt administration. A "New Deal" undertaking, it was to be a true multipurpose project. It provided badly needed jobs to more than 50,000 people, helped to control the devastating floods that periodically plagued downstream areas, aided irrigators and navigation and eventually produced hydroelectric power and provided aquatic habitat for a national wildlife refuge. The value of benefits has already greatly exceeded the project's $160,000,000 price tag.

Just below Fort Peck Dam the Missouri is joined by the Milk, named after its white coloring by the Lewis and Clark expedition. This curious river originates in the highlands of Glacier National Park and then flows northward into Alberta before returning to Montana. Water from the river is essential to the extensive irrigated agriculture in its valley, especially between Havre and Glasgow. In-stream storage at Fresno Reservoir west of Havre and off-stream storage in Nelson Reservoir east of Malta help assure the availability of waters when most needed.

Below the confluence with the Milk, the Missouri takes on little more water before flowing out of the state. It departs Montana a tamed river. As with most other Eastern Montana rivers its natural peak volume is in June, but now that month has the lowest average monthly flow and September ranks first. Much of the spring runoff is now trapped behind Fort Peck Dam and is released at a fairly steady rate during August, September, and October.

Sister river to the Missouri, the Yellowstone originates in the pristine high mountains of northwest Wyoming, flowing in a northwesterly direction into Yellowstone Lake. Leaving the lake behind, it has cut a tortuous path through Yellowstone National Park's colorful layers of volcanic rock. Over Upper and Lower Yellowstone Falls and through the beautiful Grand Canyon of the Yellowstone the river weaves its way toward Montana. It may be the yellow-colored walls of this gorge to which this river owes its name. Entering the state near Gardiner, it soon reaches the spectacular, trough-like and mountain-encircled Paradise Valley south of Livingston.

Although out of our Eastern Montana region, any major development on this reach obviously would have implications for the downstream, plains portion of the Yellowstone. One potential project that would have significant impact on the river and merits mention here is the Allenspur Dam. Power interests periodically have tested the sentiment of Montanans for this project and each time a loud chorus responds with a resounding no.

At the northern end of the Paradise Valley the river flows through a narrow hourglass-shaped constriction. Dam builders envision a 380-foot dam bridging that narrow gap and a reservoir stretching out of sight southward for more than 30 miles. Impact of such a dam and reservoir on the Yellowstone's aquatic resources would be massive. Above the dam a free-flowing and productive blue-ribbon trout stream would be replaced by a 32,000-acre lake. Downstream, modified flows would change stream morphology and alter aquatic ecosystems.

The dam has been an on-again, off-again topic for 80 years. Slopes at the potential dam site are unstable, underlying porous limestone bedrock is less than suitable, and the area is earthquake prone. Nevertheless, the project may be only dormant. With heightened downstream demands by agricultural, industrial and municipal users and growing regional electrical requirements, Montanans almost certainly will hear more about an Allenspur Dam.

A TONGUE-IN-CHEEK PROPOSAL
THE GREAT PLENTYWOOD-ALZADA HOT-DAMN DAM

A recent article in Missoula's *Western Star* carried the notion of northern Great Plains dams and reservoirs to a light-hearted extreme. In "Imagine it: Once we plug the Missouri our problems will be solved," New Yorker Tom Casey wrote:

Now if everyone would stop arguing over a niggling little valley here and a river there, we could end this waste of time. It's just hard to get the public to think big, really big. What we need to do is plug the Missouri at Williston, N.D., and build a mammoth earth dam that would stretch in a lazy arc from Plentywood, up north, to Alzada, way down south. Then let the water back up to the Continental Divide. If you can't envision the obvious benefits, you're part of the problem.

The uncertainties of dry-land farming would give way to a whole new field of aquaculture. The Little Belts, Bridgers and Crazies would become resort islands, complete with marinas. Perhaps the biggest attraction of all would be Billings, the Atlantis of the West, with a tourist-submarine base at Logan Field. . .

Worried about an expensive Northern Tier pipeline that would have to traverse earthquake zones? Forget it! We could handle all that crude with a simple trans-Montana barge line from the Port of Helena right to the Dakotas. In the winter, the traffic could be routed south to a warm-water berth over the old Gardiner hot pots.

THE CHRISAFULLI CANAL — A SECOND "YELLOWSTONE"

If the Allenspur Dam had been built, a related project may have resulted in a "second Yellowstone" paralleling the river to the north in the form of the Chrisafulli Canal. Beginning at a reservoir behind the dam, the canal would have carried water in a northerly direction and then veered eastward to enter the internally drained Lake Basin area around Rapelje. Here water could have been stored in a secondary reservoir. From there the canal would have followed the divide separating the Missouri and Yellowstone drainages, trending northeastward through the northwest corner of Rosebud County, traversing southern Garfield County and then heading toward the confluence of the Yellowstone and Missouri. The 540-mile-long project never got beyond the initial proposal stage. The cost effectiveness and problems with saline seep within the thousands of newly developed acres of irrigated farmland would make any such grandiose scheme unrealistic.

Unfettered for its entire length, the Yellowstone is the last of its kind — the sole, major, free-flowing river remaining in the contiguous United States.

Opposite: *The Yellowstone west of Columbus.* — Rick Graetz

For now the Yellowstone passes unrestricted through the narrow gap at the northern end of the valley and on to Livingston and Big Timber where it leaves a mountain dominated landscape and enters the Eastern Montana plains. It flows eastward weaving a sinuous course through a flat-bottomed and often rock-rimmed valley one to three miles wide. Giving freely of its waters, the river moves past Laurel, Billings, Forsyth, Miles City, Glendive, Sidney and a long list of other communities before joining with the Missouri just east of the North Dakota state line. This confluence marks the end of a journey that began 670 miles away. Unfettered for its entire length, the Yellowstone is the last of its kind — the sole major free-flowing river remaining in the contiguous United States.

Along that course it takes on the waters of several major rivers, all entering from the south. The Stillwater joins it near Columbus, delivering water from the rugged and majestic Beartooth Mountains. Just east of Laurel, the Clarks Fork of the Yellowstone contributes even more. It also heads in the "Roof of Montana" region draining the back side of the Beartooths and sections of Wyoming's spectacular Absaroka Range.

Lewis and Clark named the largest Yellowstone tributary the Bighorn, an approximate translation for the Indian name Ah-sah-ta, which referred to the herds of bighorn sheep in its basin. Flowing north out of Wyoming's Bighorn Basin it carries waters drained from the Absaroka and Wind River ranges to the west and the Bighorns to the east. In Montana, the waters are captured temporarily in the steepsided Bighorn Canyon behind Yellowtail Dam before continuing northward. When it joins the Yellowstone just east of Custer its flow is more than half that of the Yellowstone itself.

The Tongue and Powder are the last major tributaries to add their flows. They originate on the east flank of the Bighorn Mountains and in Wyoming's Powder River Country and carry their waters northward through one of the nation's most active coal mining districts.

Granville Stuart once commented that the Tongue was probably the "crookedest stream in Montana." Local tradition has it that the river was given this name because it was crooked like the white man's tongue. Another more plausible explanation is a tongue-like, tree covered rock outcrop near the confluence of the Tongue and Little Tongue rivers.

The Tongue's natural flow is altered by a major dam north of Decker. Water stored in the 3,500-acre Tongue River Reservoir, the second largest in the Montana portion of the Yellowstone Basin, is primarily for use by downstream irrigators. The reservoir stands in stark contrast to its engulfing dry and dusty, brown-toned landscape. If it were not in such a thinly populated area it undoubtedly would be a recreational mecca, but for now it remains essentially a private playground for resident coal miners.

Thirty-five miles downstream from Miles City and the confluence of the Yellowstone and Tongue, the Powder River dumps its silty waters into the Yellowstone. Indians called the river Powder owing to its persistent cloudiness — a consequence of the abundant shale and mudstone rocks within its basin. Although a dam has been proposed across the river at Moorhead to back water south into Wyoming, Montana's Powder River is still without a major dam or reservoir.

Increased demands on the waters of the Powder and other southeastern Montana rivers are certain to bring change. But for now, the river and the land through which it flows remain much as they have been for centuries.

Above: *Tongue River near Birney.* — Jim Romo

Below: *Powder River near Powderville.* — Rick Graetz

Left: *Bighorn canyon from Pretty Eagle.* — Rick Graetz

Below: *The Bighorn canyon before flooding was truly wild — Montana's Grand Canyon.* — Rick Graetz

BIGHORN CANYON NATIONAL RECREATION AREA

Rugged and uniquely beautiful 47-mile-long Bighorn Canyon funnels the waters of the Bighorn River northward into Montana between the precipitous eastern fault scarp of the Pryors and the western foothills of the Bighorn Mountains. Its sheer walls rise almost a quarter mile above the chasm floor exposing a colorful display of layered sedimentary rock units, capped by a red rock outcropping. Bighorn Lake behind Yellowtail Dam now floods the lowest 400 feet of these cliffs, but they still rise to awesome heights to seemingly engulf water recreationists.

The area is one of the richest archaeological sections of Montana. Evidence to date suggests aboriginal inhabitants lived in the area by at least 9,000 years ago. Ancestors of present-day Crows probably arrived around 1700. They believed that the First Maker gave them the best place in the world, including mountains, meadows, river valleys and all the beauty a people could possibly want. Out of respect for the Crows and their traditional lands, the park service does not publicize locations of religious or otherwise sacred sites. For example, the high cliffs along the west bank of the Canyon provided braves with sweeping views of the gorge and surrounding countryside and frequently were used as vision quest sites. Park visitors must view these sites from a distance.

More than 350,000 visitors used the lake and adjacent sections of the Bighorn Canyon National Recreation Area in 1980. Fishing, boating and waterskiing are popular attractions. Highways provide only limited access and a boat is essential for sightseers. When opened in 1966, plans called for a park road paralleling the reservoir through the entire park. At that time it was projected that annual park visitation would have equalled 6 million by 1985, since this would have provided another access point into the Yellowstone National Park area. Plans for the road have been dropped because of opposition by the Crow Tribe whose land would have to be crossed. Their concern centers around the loss or disturbance of religious sanctuaries, burial grounds and other archaeological sites in the pathway of the projected road. One Crow leader has compared such a project to paving a highway right through Arlington National Cemetery.

WEATHERWISE

The combination of a relatively northerly location and a situation within the continental interior insures Eastern Montana a distinctly seasonal climate. More removed by distance and blocking mountain ranges from the moderating effect of the Pacific Ocean than the western portion of the state, Montana east of the mountains experiences both the coldest winters and warmest summers. The northeastern town of Medicine Lake holds the all-time state high temperature record of 117, but also has recorded a winter low colder than 40 below zero.

Eastern Montana is probably best known for its low winter temperatures. It is not uncommon for one of the region's towns to record the nation's lowest overnight temperature (excluding Alaska). During some cold snaps, Cut Bank probably receives more national exposure than any town in Montana. To many out-of-staters, this Cut Bank Syndrome is extended to include all of Montana.

Bitterly low temperatures often accompany blasts of Canadian polar and arctic air masses as they push southward out of Canada. The effects are most pronounced in the extreme northeast where the state's lowest average January temperatures are recorded. Here towns like Glasgow, Culbertson, Medicine Lake and Wolf Point all experience average January temperatures of less than 10, and tiny Westby adjacent to the Montana-North Dakota lines claims the lowest January average at 5.7 degrees. Forty miles away, the 330 residents of Froid (French for "cold") only can guess at their mean January temperature since the town is without its own weather station.

Winter temperatures gradually moderate in a southwesterly direction and reach their highest in Eastern Montana's southwestern corner. Here, Columbus claims a January mean of 22, Billings and Roundup check in with just over 23, and Big Timber, on the fringe of Great Plains Montana, registers the highest at a balmy 27.

More moderated winter temperatures in the southwest and northward through towns like Harlowton, Lewistown, Great Falls and Choteau can be explained by several factors. Located on the western fringe of Great Plains Montana these areas are influenced more frequently by moderated Pacific air. In winter months the eastward movement of warmer Pacific air sometimes is blocked by cold air masses which may blanket the rest of Eastern Montana.

Opposite Page: *Classic anvil-shaped thunderhead near Ashland.* — Jim Romo

Top: *Prairie and east slope of the Rockies under a blanket of snow.* — Rick Graetz

Bottom: *Snowed in: Farmstead near Big Sandy.* — Ken Turner

The term blanket is especially appropriate since frigid arctic air is frequently quite shallow, sometimes only a few hundred feet thick. Because of this shallowness, surface elevations alone may restrict it to the most easterly portion of the state. Remember, Eastern Montana slopes gradually from about 5,000 feet at the base of the Rockies to 2,000 feet at the North Dakota line. A several-hundred-foot-thick blanket of cold arctic air may cover Plentywood, elevation 2,041 feet, but Great Falls, 300 miles to the west and 1,300 feet higher, may be basking in temperatures 30 to 40 degrees warmer.

Chinook Belt is the name often applied to this linear region of somewhat ameliorated winter temperatures stretching from Browning south to the Wyoming line. Chinook comes from the Indian word meaning warm wind or snow eater, and it is this wind that temporarily breaks winter's grip on the region.

Not just any movement of warm air into the belt is a chinook. A true chinook is limited to warm, westerly winter winds that have just descended the east slope of the Rockies. Air masses cool and lose moisture as they rise over the Rockies, but then heat up at a more rapid rate on their descent. In Montana the net effect is a modified air mass that is warmer and drier on the east side of the mountains than on the west. The chinook effect is strongest close to the east foot of the Rockies and generally weakens in an easterly direction.

Montana's chinooks have been responsible for spectacular rises in winter temperatures. In fact, the state holds two official national records. The 42 degree rise in temperature (minus 5 to 37) recorded at Fort Assiniboine, a former military post a few miles southwest of Havre, on January 19, 1892, still stands as the 15-minute record. Until January 1981, Kipp, near Browning, held the nation's seven-minute record. That occurred on December 1, 1896, when the temperature climbed 34 degrees. The observer also reported that a total rise of 80 degrees occurred in a few hours and that 30 inches of snow disappeared in one-half day. On January 11, 1981, Great Falls eclipsed this record when the temperature rose an incredible 47 degrees (minus 15 to 32) in just seven minutes.

> On December 1, 1892 at Kipp, near Browning, the temperature rose 34 degrees in seven minutes. The weather observer also reported a total rise of 80 degrees in a few hours and saw 30 inches of snow disappear in half a day.

When warming chinook winds are displaced quickly by surges of arctic or polar air, dramatic drops in temperature are likely. Here again, Montana holds national records. The 100-degree drop from 44 to minus 56 observed at Browning during a 24-hour period in January, 1916, has not yet been equalled. Likewise, the 12-hour record set when the temperature at Fairfield, just west of Great Falls, plummeted from 63 to minus 21 (a drop of 84 degrees) still stands.

As well as helping to explain the somewhat moderated winter temperatures in the swath of territory just east of the Rockies, and sometimes record rises and falls in those temperatures, chinooks also contribute to high average wind speeds. Mention the Windy City and most Americans automatically think of Chicago. And yet, that city's average annual wind speed is 10.3 mph compared to the 13.1 mph average at Great Falls. Residents of this Montana community are probably not interested in wresting the title of Windy City from Chicago, even though Great Falls really is the nation's windiest metropolitan area.

Above: *Tornado touches down near Stanford.* — D. L. Vaught

Opposite: *Summer storm near Forsyth.* — Jim Romo

Although Eastern Montana winters are cold by most standards, summers are predictably warm. Most of the region has an average July temperature of more than 68. Miles City checks in with the state high of 74.7 and Glendive is not far behind with its 74. The coolest summer temperatures are experienced in the higher outliers where an increase in elevation brings a corresponding drop in average temperatures.

Except for these outliers, Eastern Montana is classified as semiarid. Almost all of the region receives less than 16 inches of precipitation annually and large sections receive fewer than 12 inches. Simpson, northwest of Havre and just south of the Canadian line is Eastern Montana's lowest reporting station with an average annual precipitation of only 9.76 inches.

> Surprisingly, Eastern Montana is not the state's driest region. Strange as it may sound, Jordan receives more precipitation in an average year than does Helena, Glendive receives more than Boulder, Broadus more than Belgrade.

Most Montanans probably assume that Eastern Montana is the state's driest region, but, surprisingly, this is not the case. Even drier are some of the mountain enclosed valleys in the western portion of the state. The average annual precipitation of 9.55 inches at Dillon airport is the state's lowest, and the Helena Valley is not far behind at 10.21 inches. Strange as it may sound, in an average year Jordan receives more precipitation than Helena; Glendive more than Boulder; Broadus more than Belgrade!

The general dryness in both Eastern Montana and in some mountain enclosed valleys of western Montana is linked to a rainshadow effect. As Pacific air masses rise over Montana's Rockies, the air is cooled and its capacity to hold moisture reduced. Much of this moisture falls on the west side of the highlands and in summit areas such as in Glacier National Park where precipitation in the Continental Divide area exceeds 100 inches per year. Such mountain induced moisture is called orographic precipitation. Once over the mountain barrier, the subsiding air warms and is actually able to hold *more* moisture and thus is not as likely to release it as precipitation. Located on the lee side of this northern Rocky Mountain barrier, Eastern Montana is a classic rainshadow area.

Since the Rockies are not a single mountain ridge, but are made of a series of component mountains and intervening valleys, the same rainshadow effect explains the low precipitation totals in some of these valleys. Dillon, for example, is in the rainshadow of the Bitterroot and Pioneer mountains, and Helena is on the lee side of the main ridge of the Rockies.

Back on the plains, outliers stand out as areas with significantly higher annual precipitation. More than 40 inches per year fall on higher sections of the Big Snowy Mountains, and most other major outliers receive more than 20 inches of precipitation annually. This is also, in part, orographic moisture which results from cooling air masses, which move into the area and are forced to rise over these topographic barriers. Warm air rising from these highland areas during warmer months is another factor. Since sloping mountain flanks intercept the sun's rays more directly than surrounding flat land, they absorb more heat. Some of this heat is radiated back into the atmosphere and rises in convection currents from the highlands. Rising air cools and eventually may reach a level where condensation

and the formation of clouds take place. This helps explain why even on hot summer days outliers commonly have a crown of clouds. If sufficient rising and cooling take place, mountain showers may result. The relatively high 17.5-inch average annual precipitation at Lewistown can be attributed, in part, to orographic precipitation and convectional heating.

Like most other arid and semiarid regions in the world, precipitation in Eastern Montana varies markedly from year to year. Annual precipitation in the region rarely equals the long-term average. More commonly, it varies significantly with a grouping of wetter years often followed by a sequence of dry years and vice versa. Climatologists and meteorologists have studied this phenomenon, and it now appears that there may be some regularity to this wet-dry succession. Based on his study of Eastern Montana precipitation records and a preliminary investigation of tree rings in the region, Dr. James Heimbach of Montana State University's Institute of Natural Resources suggests that a full cycle from below-average annual precipitation to well above, and then back to low, occurs about every 20 to 25 years. Dr. Heimbach thinks this may be linked at least partly to sunspot activity, which itself has a definite cyclical pattern. Based on such a cycle, the drought starting in 1979 was "due." A better understanding of this precipitation pattern obviously would benefit the region's farmers and ranchers, who could prepare for what may be inevitable drought periods. One of the few things they can be sure of in terms of precipitation is that it won't be the same this year as it was last.

> Despite the seeming inconstancies of weather, Eastern Montana farmers and ranchers usually can count on receiving most of whatever precipitation they do get when they need it most — during the growing season.

Despite these seemingly inevitable inconstancies of weather, Eastern Montana farmers and ranchers usually can count on receiving most of whatever precipitation they do get when it is most needed — during the growing season. Long-term records show that all of Eastern Montana generally gets more than half its annual precipitation during this critical season for crops and grazing. In some areas the seasonal concentration is striking. For example, in just the first three months of the growing season, April through June, communities like Broadus, Glendive and Poplar receive almost half their average annual precipitation.

Top: *Rain for the wildflowers near Augusta.* — George Wuerthner

Opposite Page: *Yucca bloom south of Colstrip.* — Jim Romo

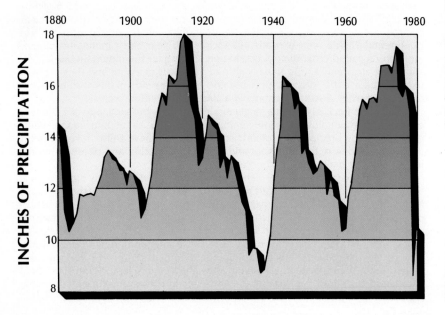

Five-year running mean averages of annual precipitation at Miles City. — Courtesy Jim Heimbach

THE VEGETATIVE MOSAIC

Eastern Montana lies on the western edge of a vast continental grassland that stretches from Texas northward into the western interior of Canada. This is the drier side of the plains, and botanists consider most of it part of the short-grass prairie. Vegetative cover within the area is characteristically bunched and sparsely distributed. It clings closely to the ground, intensifying the horizontal dimension, and amplifies the sweeping vistas that are Eastern Montana.

Most of Montana's prairie landscape is dominated by a fairly simple plant community. Vegetation is so uniform that it forces botanists dividing the grasslands into subtypes to consider minor species.

If western Montana is predominately shades of green, then Eastern Montana is buff, sand, wheat, gold and brown, with accents of green. Well before the dog days of summer the flush of green has left most of the prairie. Much to the delight of deer, but to the dismay of nighttime drivers, grasses remain greener along paved highways where runoff increases available water to roadside plant communities.

Following a succession of lengthening, dry and hot summer days, wildflowers fade, and only the hillside and mountain evergreens and the riverside cottonwood groves retain their verdant tones. This is range fire season in the sometimes tinder-dry prairie and a time when bouncing tumbleweed seems the only movement that breaks the still of the summer prairie.

If Western Montana is predominantly shades of green, then Eastern Montana is buff, sand, wheat, gold and brown with accents of green.

Man clearly has put his imprint on these prairie grasslands. Large areas have been transformed into striped grain fields and formerly weed-free prairie has been invaded by weeds that can be linked to the region's earliest homesteaders. Overgrazing by livestock may help explain the prevalence of sagebrush and saltbush in areas like the extreme southeast, northern Rosebud County, and areas around the Pryors. In the foothills of the Pryors overgrazing by horses, cattle and sheep has altered vegetation even more dramatically. There, scrub, desert-like ecosystems have replaced former semiarid grasslands.

Man clearly has put his imprint on these prairie grasslands. Large areas have been transformed into striped grain fields and formerly weed-free prairie has been invaded by weeds that can be linked to the region's earliest homesteaders.

Great Plains Montana is within a large vegetative transition zone between the heart of the plains grassland and the heavily forested Rockies. Accordingly one finds a mix of vegetation from both bordering regions. Eastern Montana may be dominated by grassland, but it is not completely without trees. In fact, there are several different types of forests in the state's eastern two-thirds.

The most luxuriant tree cover is found on higher mountain outliers, ecological islands of forests which rise from an engulfing sea of grass. Outliers not only add relief to local topography, they also introduce an obvious third dimension to the vegetative cover. In mountainous areas plant communities, as well as climate and soils, are arranged in altitudinal zones — each adapted to the progressively cooler, windier and more humid conditions that prevail with increasing altitude. Unlike the main range of the Rockies to the west, most Eastern Montana highlands are not high enough for development of subglacial or alpine tundra altitudinal zones. But according to Dr. M. Douglas Scott, Director of M.S.U.'s Institute of Natural Resources and a frequent visitor to these areas in conjunction with his ptarmigan research, summits of the Big Snowy, Pryors and Montana's Bighorns have zones of alpine tundra. They also have some subalpine forests of Engelmann spruce and Subalpine fir, but most forests on these highlands and other Eastern Montana mountains fall within the montane zone. Lodgepole pine and Douglas fir dominate these intermediate elevation forests.

Low highlands sometimes reach into the subhumid prairie parkland altitudinal belt, a transition zone between the forested zones of higher elevation and the grasslands of the semiarid plains. Here vegetation varies from prairie bunchgrass to patchy ponderosa pine. Some forests of the Northern Cheyenne Reservation, the Rosebud Mountains and Custer National Forest outside of Ekalaka qualify as prairie parkland.

What might be termed as Eastern Montana ponderosa pine savannah may be found in areas with a distinctly semiarid climate. These areas are not highlands, so orographic precipitation is not a factor. Such savannahs usually get no more precipitation than the 12 to 14 inches received by the surrounding grass-covered plains. This is sufficient moisture to support grasses like western wheatgrass or blue grama, but not ponderosa pine. Yet, ponderosa grows and, in some cases, thrives. A swath of pine savannah extends northward from the Yellowstone between Columbus and Big Timber, and another greets drivers on Interstate 94 between Forsyth and Hysham.

This apparent anomaly may have a fairly obvious explanation. Next time you drive by or through one of these savannahs, notice how they are virtually always in areas with numerous sandstone outcroppings or fractured clinker formations. Trees grow between the outcrops and sometimes right out of what appears to be solid rock. These rocks absorb little of the moisture from rain or melted snow; most of it is deflected to accumulate in associated soils and debris. This results in a micro watershed that may be several times more moist than precipitation totals suggest and wet enough to support ponderosa pine.

The Missouri Breaks scrub-pine forest occupies the riverbreaks area of the Missouri and Musselshell rivers. Here, ponderosa pine, Rocky Mountain juniper, and even Douglas fir mix with wheatgrasses, needlegrass, sagebrush and saltbush. Again, precipitation totals of only 10 to 14 inches annually would seem to rule out tree cover since these trees grow well above the river and its associated water table.

A combination of factors may help explain this scrub forest and the presence of the subhumid Douglas fir. During winters, the huge chasm that is the Breaks acts as a giant snowtrap. Howling winter winds drive snow down into the Breaks where it accumulates in massive drifts. With the warming temperatures of spring these drifts melt and charge the soils and subsurface with huge quantities of water. In places, this soil and other overburden is derived from sandstone and have the capacity to retain large amounts of water, especially when underlain by impervious shale or clay layers. The moisture is available for tree growth during subsequent months. The presence of Douglas fir may be linked to these factors, plus the fact that they grow on north-facing slopes, where shade limits moisture loss to evaporation and transpiration, and wetter ground conditions are more likely.

Top: *Off highway 200 near Winnett.* — Mark Thompson

Bottom: *Eastern Montana is shades of buff and sand colors much of the year. Overlooking the Sand Creek area south of Glendive.* — Robert Scherting

Opposite Page: *Eastern Montana possesses an amazing variety of color and vegetation; it's not at all the barren plain many imagine. Lupine and Balsamroot in a Pine park near Lame Deer.* — George Wuerthner

PRAIRIE WILDERNESS

The names Bob Marshall, Scapegoat, Great Bear, Absaroka-Beartooth, Gates of the Mountains and Selway-Bitterroot are readily recognizable as wilderness areas and are located clearly on state highway maps. But how many have heard of the U L Bend Wilderness near the confluence of the Missouri and Musselshell rivers or the Medicine Lake Wilderness southeast of Medicine Lake? To date, these two U.S. Fish and Wildlife administered areas are the only two officially designated wilderness areas in Eastern Montana. This may soon change.

All Montana wilderness areas were created under the provisions of the Wilderness Act of 1964. That legislation, however, only applied to lands administered by the U.S. Forest Service, the U.S. Fish and Wildlife Service and the National Park Service. In 1976, the Federal Land Policy and Management Act mandated a wilderness review of BLM-administered public lands for the same group of wilderness characteristics specified in the 1964 Wilderness Act. These were federal lands with the following attributes:

"(1) generally appears to have been affected primarily by the forces of nature, with the imprint of man's work substantially unnoticeable; (2) has outstanding opportunities for a solitude or a primitive and unconfined type of recreation; (3) has at least five thousand acres of land or is of sufficient size as to make practicable its preservation and use in an unimpaired condition; and (4) may also contain ecological, geological, or other features of scientific, educational, scenic or historical value."

Initial evaluation of approximately seven million acres of BLM-administered lands in Eastern Montana began in late 1978. Almost immediately some five million acres were dropped from further wilderness consideration because of obviously inappropriate qualities, leaving 1.8 million acres for intensive inventory. By early 1981 this officially had been pared to 23 Wilderness Study Areas totaling 285,000 acres. These areas are entering the study phase, in which public comment forms an integral part.

At 59,112 acres, the Bitter Creek Wilderness Study Area north of Glasgow is Eastern Montana's largest. Controversy sparked by that relatively inaccessible tract of short grass prairie and badlands typifies the emotionally charged and politically sensitive issue of prairie wilderness. For some, a grassland wilderness doesn't make any sense — who ever heard of a wilderness area without trees, they ask. Others already view the area as de facto wilderness and resent outsiders coming in and making all the fuss. Livestock interests are apprehensive about how a wilderness area would be managed and what implications that would have for grazing.

Emotions and local sentiment have run high. On a wintery December night in 1979 almost 200 people attended a BLM session on the Bitter Creek unit where a battery of locals spoke out against wilderness status. Nearby Malta has seen a 200-person, anti-Bitter Creek parade and barbeque, and as of early 1981 more than 1,200 Valley County residents had written the BLM's state office in Billings objecting to the wilderness status for the unit. Public comments, both pro and con, are encouraged by the BLM, but final designation rests with the Secretary of the Interior, Congress, and ultimately, the President.

Floodplain hardwood forests constitute yet another treed element in Eastern Montana's vegetative mosaic. Along the Missouri and the Yellowstone and their major tributaries, sinuous and broken lines of cottonwoods add visual and ecological variety to their shores. The floodplain's high water table, seasonal flooding and generally moist soils support the dominant plains cottonwood, as well as box elder, green ash, and peach leaf willow, with American elm extending as far up the Yellowstone as Dawson County.

Ranges associated with Montana's three varieties of cottonwoods clearly illustrate the transitional position of Eastern Montana's vegetation. In western Montana the black cottonwood dominates. It is the largest of the cottonwoods and grows up to 120 feet. The species also is found east of the Continental Divide within the upper drainages of both the Missouri and Yellowstone on the western fringe of the prairie. They can be spotted along the Marias, Teton and the Missouri itself as it enters the plains, as well as along the Yellowstone as far downriver as Laurel.

The medium-size narrowleaf cottonwood is limited to east-slope areas of the Rockies and has approximately the same distribution as the black cottonwood within the prairies. Except for a small area of overlap with the black cottonwood in the upper Missouri drainage, the plains cottonwood dominates river valleys further east. True sentinels of the prairie, they rise to from 60 to 90 feet above their riverside posts.

For early white settlers within this grassland-dominated landscape, these floodplain forests were often the closest source for timber. Used to build trading and military posts, fuel steamboats, and later for homesteaders' buildings, corrals and fences, these forests persisted. Now their future is less certain. Man's increasing control of river flows has reduced or eliminated seasonal flooding which evidently is necessary for cottonwood regeneration.

Especially interesting are occurrences of trees that seemingly don't belong in Eastern Montana. An example is paper birch found within two areas of southeast Montana's Custer National Forest. This is the tree Indians used to make baskets and canoes. One population encompasses about 10 acres in the Chalk Buttes and another includes trees scattered over about 30 acres in the Long Pines district of Custer National Forest. Paper birch is usually associated with cooler and wetter environments such as areas in western Montana, northern Canada or the northern Great Lakes. Custer Forest personnel manage these populations as unique vegetation sites and assume the trees are remnants of the last Ice Age when this species was more extensive.

Joe Egan, Assistant Administrator of the Wildlife Division of the Montana Fish and Game Department, reports two other distinctive occurrences in Eastern Montana. One is a population of birchleaf mountain-mahogany on sandstone bluffs in the Sarpy Creek drainage south of Hysham. The tree's normal range is the Southwest and Pacific slope areas and its presence here presents a puzzle. Most Eastern Montanans also probably would be surprised to learn that wild oak are found in Great Plains Montana. They are easy to spot south of Alzada and along the Wyoming border. These are bur oak and represent the extreme northward appendage of populations in Wyoming.

With tongue in cheek, some citizens of Great Plains Montana north of Miles City made their own forest designation. We've heard the sign has been removed. — Rick Graetz

COTTONWOOD ECOLOGY

Today's Eastern Montana cottonwood groves provide firewood and shelter for floaters and important habitat for a wide range of wildlife. Historically, a floodplain location meant that groves were periodically innundated by spring floodwaters, which were essential to a natural regeneration of its cottonwoods. Floodwaters charged soils with moisture that helped sustain trees during hot dry summer months, and deposited alluvium on the inside of river curves and in other areas adjacent to banks. Included in this sediment was nutrient-rich silt. It now appears that recently deposited alluvium, naturally fertilized by silt and saturated by floodwaters, is the primary area for cottonwood reproduction.

As a free-flowing river, the Missouri's stately cottonwood groves were a slowly renewing resource. As centuries-old trees were lost to rotting and wind damage, others were already well established. Recent investigation shows that replacement stands are lacking in many areas. This is the case within the Upper Missouri Wild and Scenic River section.

In their 1978 report entitled, A *Management Plan for the Upper Missouri Wild and Scenic River*, the Bureau of Land Management identified cottonwood groves as a major concern. They included a study pair of photos which document the loss of cottonwoods along one reach of the Missouri between 1905 and 1964. During this period major reservoirs, irrigation systems and innumerable stock dams were built to control the flow of these Missouri River waters. When these structures were built few thought to consider possible downstream consequences.

It is unlikely that dams and reservoirs will be removed and a free-flowing and periodically flooding Missouri will return. University of Montana biologist Mark Behan anticipates that the decline of the river's existing cottonwood groves will continue. To help perpetuate this vanishing resource Behan has suggested replacing lost natural seedbeds of recently deposited alluvium with carefully selected plowed small fields. Cottonwoods would be planted in them and fenced for at least 20 years to protect young trees from browsing animals. Whatever action is taken, it will have to be implemented soon if these lofty riverside woodlets are to survive.

Top: *The majestic cottonwood depends on recurrent flooding to regenerate. Seedlings,* **Below,** *thrive in flood silts.* — Mark Behan

WILDLIFE

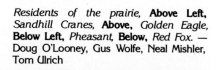

Residents of the prairie, **Above Left,** *Sandhill Cranes,* **Above,** *Golden Eagle,* **Below Left,** *Pheasant,* **Below,** *Red Fox.* — Doug O'Looney, Gus Wolfe, Neal Mishler, Tom Ulrich

Clockwise: *Rattler; Earred Grebe; Male and Female Pronghorn; Jackrabbit; Mule Deer.* — Alan Weidenrich, Tom Ulrich, Tom Ulrich, Mike Quinton, Tom Ulrich

PRONGHORN ANTELOPE

The antelope of Eastern Montana are a modern-day wildlife management success story. Prior to white settlement, Montana's antelope population may have totaled 2.5 million, most within the Great Plains portion. White settlement had an immediate and devastating affect, and by the early 1920s their numbers may have been reduced to 3,000. Numbers and range evidently began expanding steadily by the early 1930s as abandoned homesteads reverted to native vegetation. Today pronghorns are found in most sections of Eastern Montana and are popular game animals. Careful management now makes possible harvests of up to 20,000 with no threat to populations.

Montana will probably never again have the huge populations of pre-settlement times. Much of their former habitat is under the plow and other habitat use is discouraged by sheep-tight fences. In other areas sagebrush eradication programs are removing that essential antelope food. Continued modification and removal of habitat is the greatest threat to today's pronghorn population.

CHARLES M. RUSSELL NATIONAL WILDLIFE REFUGE

This is the giant of Eastern Montana wildlife refuges, comprising almost a million acres astride Fort Peck Reservoir. The refuge extends for 180 miles along Fort Peck and includes an almost unbelievable variety of wildlife habitat from native prairies, to forested coulees, cottonwood river bottoms, marshes and extensive areas of badlands.

Resident wildlife is as varied as the land itself and is a major attraction for the 120,000 visitors who enjoy the refuge each year. More than 218 species of birds alone have been identified since the refuge was established in 1936. Included are flocks of Merriam's turkeys, burrowing owls, white pelicans, great blue herons and nesting colonies of cormorant and Canada geese. From mid-April through mid-May, and again in the fall from the first of September to mid-October, scores of migratory waterfowl species swell bird populations.

Rocky Mountain bighorn sheep have been stocked to replace the extinct Audubon sheep. An initial introduction of 42 animals failed, but a 1965 transplant of 31 head resulted in a breeding population. Elk were restored to their hereditary habitat in 1951 and now the refuge and immediately adjacent areas support a huntable herd of more than 500 animals. The range also provides habitat for white-tailed and mule deer, and at least 45 different species of mammals. Indications suggest the endangered black-footed ferret also may inhabit the refuge.

PLAINS GROUSE

The Sage and Sharptail Grouse, two of Montana's six grouse species, are unique and intriguing prairie residents much admired by hunters and wildlife observers.

Both species gather in groups called leks during the month of April and for a week or two on either side of April to strut and dance. The Sage Grouse struts and the Sharptail dances. Males of both species conduct the colorful displays to attract females.

Male Sage Grouse gather year after year on the same strutting grounds where each bird occupies a carefully defined territory that probably overlaps his neighbors'. A lek containing 15 birds might occupy a space 50 yards by 50 yards. Each bird struts in a display that involves spreading the tail feathers in a fan and extending two air sacs through slits in the skin of the breast.

Sharptail Grouse dance at the same time as Sage Grouse strut, also gathering on a lek or common dancing ground. Sharptails have a number of different displays, perhaps the most remarkable of which occurs when the bird raises his tail, not fanned, to a vertical position while his body is horizontal. The yellow combs above the eyes are fully expanded, and the purple skin on each side of the neck is exposed, but not inflated. The wings are spread with the tips curved down until they nearly touch the ground. In this position, the bird rapidly stamps his feet and clicks his tail feathers. These clicks, about 45 to 50 per second, are produced by one tail feather rubbing against its neighbor. When one bird begins to dance, he quite often triggers the others around him to do the same.

Sage Grouse. — Tom Ulrich   *Sharptail Grouse.* — Tom Ulrich

THE PRAIRIE DOG

Few animals are more symbolic of Eastern Montana's short-grass plains than these gregarious, burrowing rodents. Prairie residents with a warning cry like the bark of a dog, they once were a common site standing guard atop their mounded burrow entrance.

Eastern Montana has two varieties of prairie dogs. The once widely distributed black-tailed prairie dog ranged throughout all but some northerly areas, while the white-tailed variety is restricted to southern sections of Carbon County.

Prairie dogs and their "towns" constitute an interesting element and function as a link in northern plains ecology. Although viewed as less than worthless by some individuals and the subject of extensive eradication programs, they are nevertheless important in the plains ecosystem. Their extensive tunneling and mixing of the earth aerates and enriches soil. Burrowing owls evict dogs from their burrows and use the holes for their nests. Desert cottontails also seek refuge in holes and generally are found near prairie dog towns. The rare and endangered black-footed ferret lives in the midst of prairie dogs and feeds on them almost exclusively. Mountain plovers also show a close affinity for dog towns. Even antelope frequent towns to feed on thriving forbs once the rodents have eliminated competing grasses. Attempts to rid prairie dogs from areas obviously has serious implications for these and other wildlife which share the short-grass environment.

Prairie dogs should not be confused with the more ubiquitous and smaller ground squirrel today's travelers see scampering across the road with their distinctive gait, or posed upright on highway shoulders. These are Townsends ground squirrels and it is difficult *not* to see them while driving in Eastern Montana. Prairie dogs are much rarer now owing to quite successful eradication programs. But for those interested in prairie dog watching, opportunities exist within the Charles M. Russell National Wildlife Refuge and, for those in the Great Falls area, at Ulm Pishkun State Monument.

Southeast of Big Timber, prairie dogs have their Greycliff Prairie Dog Town State Monument. This 98-acre refuge was acquired by the state in 1978 from the Nature Conservancy, a national non-profit group dedicated to preserving wild areas. By 1980 picnic tables, fencing, signs and paved roads completed the development of the park. Prairie dogs thrived within their sanctuary and by 1981 the managing Fish and Game Commission had a problem with overpopulation. As increasing numbers of prairie dogs migrated onto surrounding private lands, opposition from local ranchers grew. They complained of their children breaking out with rashes caused by prairie dog mites, economic loss owing to dogs eating crops and damage done to livestock and machinery from their burrows. In response, the commission instituted a control program and now a local rancher is responsible for eradicating dogs that wander out of the refuge.

Merriam's Turkey

Wild turkeys are probably not native to Montana; today's flocks date only from the 1950s. Encouraged by the success of turkey transplants in Wyoming, the Montana Fish and Game Department began a transplant program in 1954. Thirteen birds were obtained from Colorado and released in the Judith Mountains outside Lewistown that winter. Over the following two years additional birds from Wyoming were released near Ekalaka and outside Ashland.

The ancestral range of Merriam's turkey is the pine-oak forests of Colorado, Texas, the Southwest and Mexico. This is an open forest and often more of a savannah where patches of trees alternate with parks of grasses and associated bushes. A similar environment was afforded by Eastern Montana's scrub pine and pine savannah. Open ponderosa pine forests with rugged terrain proved ideal, and transplants thrived. The original 18 birds in the Long Pines area of Custer National Forest southeast of Ekalaka expanded to an estimated 700 in just three years. In subsequent years original flocks provided birds for transplant into other places, some of which themselves became source areas for still further transplants. The Bull Mountains and the Missouri and Mussellshell breaks received their first turkeys in 1957; the Pine Hills outside Miles City were first stocked in 1958, and by 1970 several dozen areas in both eastern and western Montana had been stocked.

There are now huntable turkey populations in six or seven areas, most in the extreme southeast corner of the state, east of the Tongue River. Fall hunting also is permitted in the Bull Mountains and the breaks area of Garfield County. There is a great deal of hunter interest in this colorful fowl, the largest of North American upland game birds.

M. Douglas Scott with wild turkey taken on the Custer National Forest near Ashland. — Dave Shors

Wild Mustangs of the Pryors

The wild mustangs of the Pryors are one of Eastern Montana's most controversial wildlife resources. About 150 horses and colts now roam the 32,000-acre Pryor Mountain Wild Horse Range and several thousand adjacent acres in southcentral Montana. Paradoxically, most visitors to this Montana range enter from the south via Lovell, Wyoming, since Montana approaches are usually strictly four-wheel-drive roads.

There is much romanticism surrounding the origin of these and other wild horses of the West, and "Bud" Brown of the Billings Bureau of Land Management office points out: "There is so much speculation that you can write a book." Bud probably knows as much about these horses as anyone and suggests they are not descendents of Spanish explorers' stock, but can more likely be traced to local Indian horses that escaped around the turn of the century.

Their relatively small size is reminiscent of the horses Indians used. An especially big stallion might weigh only 800 pounds. Blocky in nature, the Pryor horses tend toward a Spanish Barb style. According to Brown, they have five instead of six lumbar vertebrae, which gives them a shortened, more maneuverable body.

Since they retreated into an area that held little economic attraction, they were left alone and remained an island population. The 1968 creation of the Range assured their continued existence. The Wild Free-Roaming Horse and Burro Act of 1971 declares that wild horses and burros ". . . are to be considered in the area where presently found, as an integral part of the natural system of the public lands."

Earlier this century mountain lions helped control numbers, and people occasionally captured and removed some horses. Hunters and surrounding ranchers have thinned cougar populations and Wild Horse Range status forbids individuals from taking horses. Now, only disease and starvation are significant natural population regulators. In recent years these controls have proven inadequate and, although it seems at times the horses can almost "live off a rock pile," their numbers periodically have exceeded capacity of available range. This not only threatens their future, it has implications for other wildlife, including mule deer which share some of the same winter range.

The Bureau of Land Management would like to have encouraged natural predators such as the mountain lion, but ranchers have resisted, fearing loss of their own livestock. To date, the major population control has been the federal Adopt-a-Horse program. In 1973 a roundup netted some 20 horses, and as recently as 1980 five head were removed from the range. Captured horses are made available free of charge to the public who need only cover associated veterinarian costs, although a new policy under consideration would charge recipients up to $200 per horse. Most horses now find new homes with people in Montana and Wyoming.

EASTERN MONTANA YESTERDAY

Eastern Montana, like any other region, cannot be understood without a consideration of its past. There, and everywhere, much of what we have today is really only a composite or mosaic of vestiges and remnants of former times. Even the character and personality that is Eastern Montana obviously did not appear instantaneously in the 1980s. Roots lie both in the place and deep in the region's chronicle of human history.

There seems to have been a tendency for popular histories to skim over the pre-history of Montana, as if Lewis and Clark actually discovered an uninhabited land. So, if after beginning to read the section that follows, you ask yourself "what's with all this early man stuff, let's get to the cowboys and Indians," consider the following: people probably have been living in Eastern Montana for at least 12,000 years. If that time span were concentrated into a 24-hour day, the Lewis and Clark expedition did not enter the picture until about 21 minutes til midnight!

No one knows when the first men stepped into what is now Eastern Montana. So far archaeologists haven't found that unarguable site that says "these were the *first* Montanans and they lived here at such and such a time." This site will obviously never be found. Rather, the story undoubtedly will continue to unfold as individual finds add bits and pieces of new information.

Buried beneath the plains of Eastern Montana may lie archaeological remains that, because of the area's strategic location, could help solve the riddle of the peopling of the North American continent. The chronicle probably began on the frozen margin of western Alaska during the last great Ice Age. Most authorities acknowledge the Bering Land Bridge, or Beringia, as the portal by which the first people entered the Americas. At that time large amounts of the world's water were frozen and sea level was lowered by as much as several hundred feet. The narrow Bering Strait disappeared and North America and Asia were joined by a strip of land linking Alaska's Seward Peninsula with Siberia over which humans and animals could have crossed from Asia to North America. A lowering of sea level and

land bridge may not even have been necessary since many may have trekked across on winter pack ice which even today sometimes clogs the strait.

These new arrivals entered a continent still in the grip of the Ice Age, with much of its northern half frozen and buried under ponderous glaciers. Understandably, these Stone Age hunters eventually headed south toward warmer climes. Some archaeologists favor a migration through a periodically open ice free corridor along the east foot of the Rockies. Evidently, glaciers that spilled out of the mountains retreated to the west and the continental ice sheet withdrew easterly, thereby opening a passageway. This corridor would have directed early migrants southward into Montana, where thousands of years ago the very first American may have stepped across what is now the Alberta-Montana border north of Cut Bank.

Even if this scenario is correct, the record is still unclear as to when the migration occurred. Archaeological sites are often controversial and subject to individual interpretation. Dating techniques may be questioned, uncertainty about whether a site has been disturbed and arguments over whether "artifacts" are man-made lead to lively debate among archaeologists and help explain the lack of consensus. Some scholars are not convinced there is any conclusive evidence of people in the New World until 12,000 years before the present (BP). Others are equally sure that we were here by about 30,000 BP and some will not be surprised if evidence eventually surfaces that verifies human presence somewhere in the Americas by 100,000 BP!

So far, the earliest accepted evidence of man in Montana dates from about 11,500 BP and comes from just beyond the western edge of our Eastern Montana region. This is the nationally signficant Anzick, or Wilsall, Site north of Livingston. Like so many other sites, it, too, has controversial elements. Still, it may be the most ancient archaeological find in Montana to date. Few residents outside of the state's small community of archaeologists are aware of this extraordinary find, which produced one of the largest stone implements ever discovered in the nation and may represent the earliest evidence of religion anywhere in the New World.

Above: *The Anzick site near Wilsall, helping document man's presence in Montana 11,500 years ago.* — Larry A. Lahren

Middle: *A very large cleaver and,* **Right:** *Clovis-Man tool kit.* — Tim Antonsen, Livingston Enterprise, Larry A. Lahren

THE ANZICK SITE

The Anzick discovery was totally happenstance and may never have occurred if it weren't for the 1968 construction of Wilsall's new high school. That spring Calvin Sarver and his cousin, Ben Hargis, were employed loading stone on the Melvyn Anzick property north of Livingston for use in a drain field at the town's new school. Hargis was scooping a load of rock from the base of a talus slope into a front-end loader when he noticed something strange fall to the base of the slope. He immediately realized that it was a stone artifact. Both men quit working and frantically started picking other stone and bone artifacts out of a spot about four feet up the face of the slope.

Sarver recalls that all the artifacts came from within about a three-foot area and were all covered with red ochre, "like they had been stored in it." Some human bone fragments also were found and he recalls that they may have come from a little higher up. Reflecting back to that day, Sarver remembers thinking that it looked as if the artifacts and human bone "had once sat on some sort of ledge and the whole thing had broken and fallen off . . . like maybe it had once been the floor of a cave." Neither man realized the true significance of their find, but they got a hint when they reported their discovery to a local amateur archaeologist who "about had a heart attack," as Sarver put it.

Soon after the discovery, a research team from the University of Montana investigated the site, but concluded that disturbance by Hargis and Sarver and the unscientific method of excavation would make interpretations suspect.

In 1971 Dr. Larry A. Lahren, contract archaeologist with his Livingston-based Anthro Research, and Dr. Robson Bonnichsen, then with Canada's National Museum of Man in Ottawa, began their investigation of what has become known as the Anzick Site. After careful field work, including several test pits and trenches, they came to some startling conclusions which since have been accepted by some other experts in the field.

They concluded that even though disturbed by Hargis and Sarver, the artifacts and human skeletal remains were from the same period, and the site constitutes the first known Clovis burial. The name Clovis refers to a type of stone projectile point with a distinctive fluted base, perhaps added to facilitate attachment to a shaft.

These points have been found in sites that consistently date from 11,000 to 12,000 years ago. The term, Clovis, since has come to refer to the points, this period and the culture of these mammoth-hunting Paleo-Indians.

Dr. Lahren thinks the Anzick discovery may have been a secondary burial. That may explain the fact that only a few human bones, including most of a skull, some vertebrae, a few rib fragments and a clavicle were found. The entire assemblage of tools was covered in red ochre, perhaps suggesting some sort of burial ritual.

The more than 90 bone and stone artifacts, presumably buried with the human remains, represent the most complete Clovis tool kit yet discovered. Some had never been used. One might speculate that tools were left to help assure the deceased successful hunts in an afterlife. Every necessary tool for mammoth killing and processing was there — bone foreshafts which could be attached to a shaft and tipped with a sharp projectile point for use as a lance, large serrated-edge biface artifacts that might be used for sawing through bone, long gouges and chisels for removing flesh from hide and even a gigantic cleaver for dismembering a mammoth carcass.

The Anzick Site is especially exciting because of new insight it has provided on the Clovis culture. It constitutes what may be the earliest evidence of religion yet discovered anywhere in the New World. By at least 9,500 B.C. these Paleo-Indians of Eastern Montana apparently wondered about life after death and had respect for the supernatural. Implements were made of stone that can be traced to several quarry sites, including one in Wyoming. According to Dr. Lahren, this may suggest that by at least 11,500 BP these people had established trade links that reached beyond Montana's present borders. Since long-distance trade ties probably developed over an extended period of time, this may mean that early man in Eastern Montana predates the Anzick Site by many generations.

The huge cache of bone and stone artifacts found were those of Paleo-Indians. These people lived on the fringes of the retreating ice sheet in an Eastern Montana that was both cooler and wetter than today. The tools they left were uniquely suited to slaying and processing their primary quarry — giant 15-foot-tall mammoths. The bow and arrow had not yet appeared in North America, so these Gargantuan beasts had to be felled at close range with stone-tipped lances and spear-throwers. Other Ice Age animals, such as now extinct species of bison and camel, probably were hunted also, but these Indians' livelihood was based on pursuit of the mammoth. Its meat and marrow provided food, hides were used for shelter, and bone became raw material for tools.

By at least 7,500 years ago the cool and wet environment associated with the waning of the Ice Age is thought to have gradually yielded to much drier conditions. Life forms changed, the gigantic Ice Age animals disappeared, and human residents of Eastern Montana had to adapt their life style in order to continue living in the area. Meso-Indians of this later period shifted emphasis from big game hunting to a dependence on smaller animals, like deer and rabbits, and began relying more on gathering of roots, seeds. and berries. This form of existence was coupled with an intensification of human occupancy and probably persisted until several thousand years ago. And then another change in the natural environment offered new opportunities to which early residents again adjusted.

Around that time, the range and population of the plains bison gradually expanded. Eventually, numbers reached levels that helped assure plains people a reliable food supply as well as useful hides and bones. Indians gradually shifted to an increased dependence on bison hunting. A distinct plains Indian culture centered on the buffalo developed.

These later plains Indians included those present in Montana at the time of white contact. Like the white man and their paleo predecessors, they, too, were migrants from other areas. Anthropologists and archaeologists do not agree on when and from where these more recent tribes arrived. Some theorists put at least some modern plains tribes in Eastern Montana as far back as 2,000 years ago; others are not convinced that any of the present tribes were there before 1600.

By the middle 19th century Eastern Montana was dominated by five major tribes. The powerful Blackfeet nation controlled the most extensive territory, claiming all of the western half north of the Yellowstone. South of that river was home to the much less numerous Crow, who called themselves the "Absarokee," from "absa" meaning large beaked bird, and "rokee' meaning children or offspring. This large beaked bird is assumed to be the raven, which closely resembles the somewhat smaller crow. Both tribes were rich in horses, which partly explains their constant intertribal warfare. The home of the "bird people" also abutted against the land of the Cheyenne, which lay roughly east of Rosebud Creek. They probably once occupied an area astride the present-day Minnesota-Wisconsin border and gradually shifted westward, arriving in Montana in the 1830s. Cheyenne territory included what is now Montana's southeastern corner. To the north, Assiniboine lands reached into Montana from the north and east. These people also moved into the area from further east, and may have started their westward migration in the 1600s from the pine forested area north of Lake Superior. Wedged between these latter two tribes and the Blackfeet were the hunting lands of the Atsina, or Gros Ventre. By at least the early 1800s, their movement had carried them from Minnesota to northcentral Montana, where they allied themselves with their powerful Blackfeet neighbors to the west.

The northern Great Plains of Montana onto which these Indians moved was among the most bountiful buffalo regions on the continent. Bison provided an abundant source of both food and materials and became central to plains Indian culture. But without use of the horse until approximately the mid-1700s, these pedestrian residents had to rely on their ingenuity to assure the adequate supply of buffalo meat, hides and bones so critical to their subsistence. Certainly as early as 2,000 years ago, prehistoric inhabitants of Eastern Montana, predecessors of the later tribes, had developed two effective communal systems for bison kills — the buffalo jump and the pound.

Buffalo jumps, where Indian hunters stampeded herds off the face of a cliff, were most common in the western portion of the plains. There, nature's rugged and

MONTANA'S GREAT PLAINS INDIANS

Page 46 . . . .

Clockwise from Upper Left: *Sioux couple at Crow Agency; Plenty Coups, last chief of the Crow; Cree boy on the Rocky Boys Reservation; Bull's Head, Gros Ventre on the Ft. Belknap Reservation, 1906; Standing Rattle, Assiniboine; Piegan camp on the Teton River above Ft. Benton, 1884; Fourth of July dance at Crow Agency, 1894.* — Montana Historical Society.

broken topography provided more cliffs for potential jump sites. Migratory buffalo were naturally attracted to the plains' western fringe, with its deeply incised river valleys that afforded herds protection from harsh winter winds, and where chinooks moderated winter temperatures, often exposing grasses for grazing. Ideal jump sites had vertical drops ranging from 30 to 50 feet. Shorter drops did not always result in sufficient impact to kill or maim, and much higher cliffs tended to splatter the animals.

In addition to an acceptable height, an adjacent grazing area was another prerequisite. At the best jump sites, these grassy plains to which buffalo were attracted converge toward a cliff. The Indians accentuated the funneling effect of the grassy expanses by building V-shaped drive lanes of two converging stone walls about three feet tall. Buffalo were driven from the grazing area, stampeded through the chute-like drive lane and over the cliff. The animals, either killed or maimed by the fall, piled up at the base of the cliff ready for skinning and butchering.

The pound-type bison kill was another specialized variety of drive and almost certainly was more common. Instead of stampeding animals over a cliff, the Indians drove them from the grazing area and down a short, steep slope. There they funneled the buffalo through a stone-enclosed drive lane which directed the herd into a pound, or slaughter pen, where Indians used spears, arrows and later, guns, to kill the animals.

ULM PISHKUN BUFFALO JUMP

The Blackfeet called their buffalo jumps "pishkun," and it seems appropriate that the jump four miles north of Ulm be called Ulm Pishkun. Located just 12 miles west of Great Falls, this pishkun may have been used as early as 900 A.D. It is now protected as a state monument where today's visitors still can sense the drama and excitement of thundering herds of buffalo being driven from the west and down the main 30-foot precipice.

At jumps like Ulm Pishkun that were used over long periods, thick layers of bone and carcass meal, containing arrowheads used to kill maimed animals, accumulated at the base of the cliff. Successive layers of charred bone fragments suggest that carcass remains were burned prior to a new drive. In the spring of 1947, well before designation as a state monument, the upper 12 feet of this bone deposit were bulldozed for use as fertilizer. The excavator calculates he obtained about 150 tons of bone and carcass meal. Most of this zone was homogeneous bone deposits, but at greater depth bone layers were mixed with increased amounts of soil, suggesting the jump was at first used only intermittently and then with increasing frequency.

Prior to its excavation, the base of this jump, like many others probably supported a lush vegetative cover, greened and thickened by the ultra fertile soil which was fed by decaying piles of bone and carcass. Even today jumps and pounds are sometimes detectable from a distance in the spring when overlying grass turns greener sooner than surrounding vegetation.

It is clear that the 100-foot-wide pishkun on the south side of tongue-like Taft Hill Plateau was the most frequently used of several in the immediate vicinity. Bone deposits at several places along the base of the same cliff, including a medium-size one a mile away on the north face of the plateau, evidently were alternate jumps, some of which may have been used only once. At the base of the main jump is evidence of a refuse basin. It contained a quantity of mostly long bones that had been crushed for their marrow. Associated fire hearths show that rendering produced grease for use in cooking and making pemmican.

Like many other jumps, Ulm Pishkun has associated occupation areas as evidenced by tipi rings and additional hearths. A main campsite was located about 50 yards away from the base of the jump, adjacent to a small spring. This site has produced additional arrow points as well as stone knives, scrapers, stone choppers and some pottery.

For Montana's plains Indians, buffalo-procuring methods changed dramatically around the mid-18th century when they acquired the horse. The animal and its use gradually had been diffusing northward from the Spanish in the Santa Fe area, and finally reached the northern plains Indians after passing through several intermediary tribes.

Acquisition of the horse, coupled with the adoption of guns obtained directly or indirectly from French and British fur traders to the north, revolutionized life styles. Rather than lying in wait for buffalo at grazing areas associated with their jumps and pounds, equestrian Indians now also could pursue the beasts wherever they were found. This assured an even more reliable food supply.

The horse made these already nomadic people even more mobile. Previously, dogs were the primary beasts of burden. When it was time to move camp, portable

Lithograph from U.S. Government Railroad Survey of the mid-1850s — Courtesy John Alwin

tipis were disassembled and dog travois were loaded with the buffalo-hide coverings and poles. Horse travois made moves much easier and quicker.

Mounted on horses and armed with guns, plains Indians became even more formidable warriors. In a few short decades white trappers and fur traders would be scouring the Indian lands of Eastern Montana. They would become the first white men to realize the fury of these tribes once they sensed a threat to their lands and their life styles.

THE TIPI

Like other nomadic people past and present, the plains Indians of Eastern Montana needed a movable shelter. The Bedouins of North Africa had their tents, the Mongols of Asia, their yurts, and the plains Indians of North America, their tipis. The name is from the Sioux and is formed by "ti," meaning to dwell or live, and "pi," meaning used for. This familiar conical shelter traditionally was built with a covering of buffalo hides stretched over a cone-shaped frame of poles. An average-size tipi with a diameter of 14 to 16 feet required a covering made from 12 to 14 tanned hides.

An authentic tipi was always a tilted cone, steeper up the back. If the cone had no tilt, smoke from winter fires would have to be vented out the tip of the structure, where poles converged. Keeping rain and snow out of such an opening in wet weather would be difficult. To rectify this problem, tipi cones were tilted, and a smoke flap was cut into the covering just below the converging poles on the longer, front side, above the entryway. Each wing-like smoke flap was held open by a pole. These flaps easily could be overlapped when necessary to keep out precipitation.

Inside, tipis generally were lined up to a height of 5 or 6 feet with a hide liner which served several essential roles. First, it kept wind entering under the base of the tipi from creating drafts across the living space. Outside air was deflected up the lining and then toward the center of the tipi, providing ideal ventilation for the central fire. The lining also directed moisture that dripped down the poles away from the inhabitants.

In addition, the air space between the lining and the outside tipi cover provided insulation that helped keep the tipi warm in winter and cool in summer. The lining also prevented the casting of shadows from the central fire onto the outer tipi covering. More than modesty was involved, since a moving shadow might become a target for an enemy lurking outside. One additional bonus: painted and decorated, these linings brightened the atmosphere inside the shelter.

The tipi provided a nearly ideal shelter for the migratory plains Indians. It was quick and easy to erect and take down, was portable and could be built with readily available materials. As a home it was comfortable and roomy, and kept its occupants warm in winter and cool in summer. As its name suggests, the tipi was used to *live* in, unlike the tents of today's outdoorsmen.

The tipi is now essentially absent from the Eastern Montana landscape. It still can be viewed, however, on exhibit at some Eastern Montana museums. The largest concentration can be seen each summer at the annual Crow Fair, when hundreds of tipis erected for the festival make Crow Agency the Tipi Capital of the World.

Top: *At a festival on the Blackfeet Reservation* — Homer Collins

Bottom: *Montana mixture: Modern home on the Crow Reservation with tipi poles ready for a powwow.* — John Alwin

French explorers and fur traders may have been the first white men to enter Montana. In January of 1743, two sons of Pierre Gaultier de Varennes, Sieur de La Verendrye are thought to have visited what is now southeastern Montana. Francois and Louis Joseph had been sent by their father in search of a reputed water route to the Pacific. They fell short of that objective, but reportedly did see the "Shining Mountains" and encountered the "Bow People." The mountains the brothers sighted may have been the Bighorns and the Indians, the Crow, but since their journal of the expedition is sketchy and lacking in specifics on locations, we only can presume they reached Montana.

It seems unlikely that other white men did not visit Eastern Montana during the next half century. It is not difficult to picture grizzled and buckskinned free traders drifting south out of the British lands to the north or westward up the Missouri from its lower reach. Lured by hope of huge profits from a virgin fur area, these may have been the first men to set traps along Eastern Montana's waterways. That they evidently failed to leave written accounts of their exploits is not surprising since probably few, if any, were literate. Verbal accounts of their expeditions may have been merely shrugged off in St. Louis as just more fur traders' braggadocio. Or perhaps they were discreet and did not reveal their source area so as not to invite competition.

The beginning of systematic exploration of Eastern Montana had to await the celebrated Lewis and Clark expedition of 1804-06. Conceived by Thomas Jefferson before he became president, and even before America's 1803 purchase of the Louisiana Territory, the expedition conveniently divides prehistory and history within Eastern Montana.

Just beyond the mouth of the "Roche Jaune" or Yellowstone, Montana was entered from the east on April 26, 1805, as the Corps of Discovery moved up the Missouri enroute to the Pacific. Their voyage carried them through the awe-inspiring Breaks and westward where they began sighting Rocky Mountain outliers and finally the Rockies themselves. Beyond the Marias they became the first white men of present record to view and describe the thundering Great Falls of the Missouri. On July 18 the entourage passed through the Missouri's defile in the Adel Mountains, leaving our Eastern Montana region behind.

The expedition continued westward and succeeded in reaching the Pacific in early November. After wintering over at their newly erected Fort Clatsop, the party began the return journey the following spring.

South of present-day Missoula Captains Lewis and Clark separated into two main parties to permit exploration of a larger area. Lewis crossed the Continental Divide and then dropped down onto the plains via the Sun River. A side trip took him and several other men up the Marias where a terrifying encounter with a party of Blackfeet (Piegan) warriors ended with the killing of two Indians. Lewis and his party quickly departed by horse, crossing 100 miles of rugged terrain in just 18 hours! Once back at the Missouri, Lewis rejoined other members of his party and retraced their route of the previous spring, this time floating downriver, back to the mouth of the Yellowstone.

Meanwhile, Captain Clark had led his party south up the Bitterroot River, across Gibbon's Pass, south through the Big Hole Valley and northeastward to the Three Forks of the Missouri. From here the party moved eastward across the Gallatin Valley and reached the Yellowstone River near present-day Livingston via Bozeman Pass. Clark and his party floated down the Yellowstone in two dugouts, enjoying the most comfortable and leisurely traveling of the entire expedition.

Great Falls of the Missouri before the dams. F. Jay Haynes photo, 1880. — Courtesy, Montana Historical Society

Enroute Clark stopped to carve his name and date in a rock formation he christened Pompey's Pillar, after Sacajawea's child whom he called, "my boy Pomp." The party reached the Missouri in mid-summer where they rejoined Lewis's party further downstream.

Lewis and Clark left behind an Eastern Montana that never again would be the same. General aspects of the regional geography had been surveyed, and definitive scientific observations and actual field samples added more valuable information on this former *terra incognita*. Previously, the only maps of the area had been crude drafts based on sketchy information obtained from the Indians. The expedition provided the information needed to fill in large map voids and, for example, to replace dotted courses of presumed rivers with known watercourses. And except for the Blackfeet, the Corps of Discovery initiated friendly contact with every group of native people encountered. But perhaps even more significant than these monumental accomplishments was their proclamation that the country through which they passed was richer in beaver than any other place on earth. This pronouncement served as a catalyst for the American fur trade of the Far West. As the entourage descended the Missouri they encountered several parties of trappers heading upriver — a trickle that would eventually swell to a steady stream of trappers and traders who extended the American fur trade frontier into Eastern Montana.

> The Lewis and Clark expedition may have suggested the potential for a major American trade in the upper Missouri region, but Manuel Lisa ignited the spark that commenced the trade.

A colorful era in Eastern Montana's history was taking root. It was the time of now legendary adventurers like John Colter and Jim Bridger. Competition was keen for the riches of this prime fur region. Fur companies soon vied with individuals and loosely knit groups for the region's sought-after beaver pelts. The Missouri Fur Company, American Fur Company and Rocky Mountain Fur Company were some of the larger corporations that pushed trade into the region under the leadership of now historic figures including Manuel Lisa, John Jacob Astor and William H. Ashley.

Large-scale trading within Eastern Montana was inaugurated in 1807. That year Manuel Lisa led an expedition of about 50 men upriver from St. Louis and built Manuel's, or Lisa's, Fort at the confluence of the Yellowstone and Bighorn rivers. While the Crows traded at the fort that winter, white trappers fanned out to work other tributaries of the Yellowstone, Bighorn, Powder and Tongue rivers. Meanwhile, John Colter's sojourn carried him beyond these rivers and his fellow trappers and perhaps into today's Yellowstone National Park where his sightings of strange natural wonders earned the place the name, Colter's Hell. Lisa returned to St. Louis the following spring heavily laden with furs and enthusiastic about the fur potential of the upper Missouri-Yellowstone country. Skeptics could question mere reports of a fur El Dorado, but even doubters couldn't deny the mounds of pelts Lisa unloaded on the St. Louis docks. The Lewis and Clark expedition may have suggested the potential for a major American trade in the upper Missouri region, but Manuel Lisa ignited the spark that commenced the trade.

Eastern Montana was not immediately innundated by an invasion of trappers, or blanketed with a dense network of trading posts. There were successful expeditions and other posts were built, but it was not until the 1820s and 1830s that

> Two decades of relentless trapping by Indians and white men caused beaver populations to plummet by the early 1830s.

the Americans began to more fully exploit the region's fur resources. Hostility of the Blackfeet, the War of 1812, and disruption of markets were just some of the factors that tempered earlier efforts. The Blackfeet forcibly kept trappers and traders out of their territory until the early 1830s, but by the mid-30s even that most resistant nation allowed the American Fur Company to add Fort McKenzie near the mouth of the Marias. The American Fur Company dominated the upper Missouri trade, which by then had begun shifting from small fur bearers to buffalo.

More than two decades of relentless trapping by Indians and white men caused beaver populations to plummet by the early 1830s. Even if numbers had remained stable in the upper Missouri country, a change in clothing styles in Europe meant little market for these once highly regarded pelts. Trade emphasis shifted to the northern plains' larger, more easily obtained, and seemingly limitless supply of buffalo.

Although Indians continued to trap and kill small animals for pelts that they traded at the white man's posts, they increasingly turned to dealing in buffalo robes. By the mid-1830s, the Blackfeet were trading 10,000 robes annually at Fort McKenzie alone, and by 1841 the post's production had more than doubled.

The fur traders were interested only in robes of cows or young bulls killed when the animals had their thick winter coats. Before they would be taken in trade, hides had to be dressed, a job relegated to squaws. One woman could process only about 30 robes per winter, making this the limiting factor in the robe trade. So lucrative were potential profits to the Indians, that the practice of polygamy evidently became more prevalent among these plains tribes.

By the 1840s the buffalo trade was well established, having progressed to the point where steamboats were employed to ferry supplies and pelts between St. Louis and Fort Union, located on the Missouri just east of the present Montana-North Dakota state line. Since Indians did most of the work, few white traders were required. Posts like Fort McKenzie, Fort Cass at the strategic juncture of the Yellowstone and Bighorn rivers and, after 1846, Fort Benton, served as depots and collection points for the trade, and each might have had a complement of 50 to 100 men.

> In 1837 the crew of an American Fur Company steamboat carried smallpox upriver to Fort Union. The epidemic quickly spread westward, ravaging thousands. The Assiniboine were reduced from 1,000 to 400 lodges within a year, and the Blackfeet may have lost half or more of their people.

Even though the number of white traders in Eastern Montana was small, their impact on the plains Indians with whom they dealt was profound. These and earlier traders introduced diseases that decimated tribes. In 1837 the crew of an American Fur Company steamboat carried smallpox upriver to Fort Union. The epidemic quickly spread westward, ravaging thousands. The Assiniboine were reduced from 1,000 to 400 lodges within a year and the Blackfeet may have lost half or more of their people. Perhaps even more devastating to Indian societies than fatal disease was extensive use of alcohol in the trade. Despite an 1832 ban on alcohol as a trade item, it remained an essential element of commerce.

The fur trade still held sway in Eastern Montana when the steamship *Chippewa* reached Fort McKenzie, just above the mouth of the Marias, in 1859. Steamboats had been plying the Missouri River out of St. Louis since the early '30s, but none ever had navigated that far beyond Fort Union. The next year two steamboats continued beyond Fort McKenzie and on to Fort Benton. Their arrival symbolized the onset of yet another era in the Eastern Montana chronicle. One by one, fur posts were abandoned with only Fort Benton succeeding in making the transition from post to permanent settlement. Cargoes indicative of a maturing frontier region became increasingly more common. In a few short years Fort Benton would be the bustling entrepôt for a booming western gold mining district and would blossom into Eastern Montana's first town.

In 1864 Montana was granted territorial status and organized into its original nine counties. Territorial population totaled some 20,000 whites, but most were concentrated in the gold-rich valleys of the southwestern corner. More than half of Eastern Montana fell within gigantic Big Horn County and most of the remainder was encompassed in sprawling Choteau, Deer Lodge and Gallatin counties.

While numerous young communities dotted the map of western Montana by the mid-1860s, Fort Benton remained the only "town" within the territory's plains portion. This was still Indian country where Blackfeet, Crow, Assiniboine and neighboring tribes greatly outnumbered resident whites. At this time there was little to make Eastern Montana a destination for settlers. It lacked the mineral wealth of the territory's west, agriculturalists saw little potential in an area that was without transportation to essential markets, and hostile Indians made even passing through the area a dangerous undertaking.

During the 1860s and 1870s Eastern Montana was largely a transit region, an area merely to be crossed enroute to more promising areas further west. By the early 1860s immigrant movement across the region was funneled along three major routeways. Perhaps least arduous was steamship travel up the Missouri to Fort Benton where the Mullan Wagon Road allowed travelers to continue into western Montana, Idaho and Washington.

To the north lay the Northern Overland Route, or Minnesota-Montana Road, which had carried immigrants under military escort as early as 1862. It provided hopeful emigrants from the northern states with a closer and more convenient alternative than the Oregon Trail. From Fort Union the route paralleled the Missouri on the north, ascended the Milk River Valley and cut south to Fort Benton just west of the Bear Paw Mountains.

For travelers on the Oregon Trail, the Bozeman Cutoff, or Bozeman Trail, provided direct access to the gold fields of Western Montana.

For travelers on the Oregon Trail, the Bozeman Cutoff, or Bozeman Trail, provided direct access to the gold fields of western Montana. John Bozeman and John Jacobs are credited with laying out the route in 1863. It pulled away from the Oregon Trail east of present-day Casper, Wyoming, entered Montana south of today's Wyola, and then veered west. Once immigrants crested Bozeman Pass the trail carried them on to Virginia City and the surrounding mining districts.

The Bozeman may well be Montana's most celebrated immigrant trail despite the fact that it carried few civilian travelers and was used regularly for only a few years. Its notoriety undoubtedly can be linked to headline-garnering Sioux and Cheyenne attacks, the first significant Indian raids on settlers enroute to Montana. The military post of Fort C. F. Smith in Montana, and two other forts along the Bozeman Cutoff in Wyoming were established to protect travelers using the trail, but after two more years of continued Indian trouble the trail was closed and the forts abandoned in 1868.

Top Left: *The steamboat "De Smet" at Fort Benton Levee c. 1870s.* — Courtesy, Montana Historical Society

Bottom Left: *Freighter's outfit, 1882 near Coulson-Billings.* — Courtesy, Montana Historical Society

Above: *1867 Map of Montana. Note that most of Eastern Montana was contained in three counties.* — Courtesy, John Alwin

The Indian-white conflicts along the Bozeman were a prelude to what would be a decade and a half of sporadic hostilities ranging from small skirmishes to full-pitched battles. In this brief period a frontier army wrestled final control of land from aboriginal inhabitants who fought bravely to defend their home and the only way of life they had ever known. The names of heroes on both sides are readily recognizable — military officers Custer, Terry, Miles, Benteen and Gibbon; and legendary chiefs including Sitting Bull, Crazy Horse, Lame Deer and Joseph. Surprisingly, most of the great battles of Eastern Montana took place in the span of only five years between 1873 and 1877. The most famous is clearly the 1876 Battle of the Little Big Horn. In this most studied and analyzed Indian battle in American history, Major General George Armstrong Custer and five companies of the 7th U.S. Cavalry, more than 200 men, died at the hands of an overwhelming number of Sioux and Cheyenne.

By 1880 the famous Indian battles of the '70s were history. The buffalo so central to traditional Indian lifestyles were nearing extinction and the once-proud red men of the plains were relegated to an almost universally pathetic life on their progressively shrinking reservations. There had been a conflict of cultures and theirs was the loser.

Above: *Fort Assiniboine, morning guard mount.* — Courtesy, Montana Historical Society

Left: *General George A. Custer.* — Courtesy, Montana Historical Society

54

CUSTER BATTLEFIELD NATIONAL MONUMENT

The only fact some Americans know about Eastern Montana is that this is where Custer made his historic last stand. Today the site of that famous Indian battle is part of an 800-acre national monument administered by the U.S. Park Service. It is a popular tourist stop, attracting thousands each year. At the monument, Americans as well as foreigners from as far away as Japan and West Germany all seem eager to see firsthand the site of an historic event they have heard about since they were children.

The monument comprises two detached portions, linked by the 4½-mile-long Battlefield Road. The northern component includes Custer Hill, where on June 26, 1876, Custer and the remnants of the five companies under his immediate command made their last stand. A cluster of 52 weathered white marble tablets on the hillside among the tall prairie grasses show where the last cavalry troopers fell. Atop the hill a memorial shaft marks the common grave for enlisted men who lost their lives in this controversial battle.

A combination visitor center-museum is located at the base of Custer Hill. It contains dioramas and other exhibits relating to the battle, plains Indian culture and the life of frontier soldiers of the 1870s. The Custer Battlefield National Cemetery lies next to the visitors center. Its row upon row of simple white headstones are a reminder that the entire battlefield was maintained as a National Cemetery under the U.S. Army until 1940.

Narrow and winding Battlefield Road carries visitors south from the Custer battle site to the Reno-Benteen Battlefield. For maximum benefit, park personnel suggest that visitors first stop at the visitor center to obtain basic information and then proceed to the Reno-Benteen site to begin their tour.

Since this battlefield involves a lesser known aspect of the conflict, a brief explanation may be in order. After locating the Indian village on June 25, Custer divided his 700-man 7th Cavalry. He took five companies; Captain Frederick W. Benteen was charged with three; and Major Marcus A. Reno commanded the remaining three companies.

The village included 10,000 to 12,000 people and constituted one of the largest gatherings of Indians in northern plains history. Its 2,500 to 4,000 warriors were several times the expected maximum force.

Custer led his men down the east side of the Little Bighorn and into history. Meanwhile, Reno and his company were repelled by an Indian attack on the west side of the river and were forced to retreat. They moved southeast across the river where they took up a defensive position on bluffs within this second battlefield site. Reinforced by Benteen and his men they held off repeated attacks during that day and into the next. When the Indians finally retreated, they left the combined Reno-Benteen force with 47 fatalities and 52 wounded. A 7th Cavalry Memorial now marks the site of this lesser known secondary battle.

Park officials are concerned that billboards, flashing neon signs, and hot dog stands may soon mar the integrity of this historical site. Battlefield Road linking the two parcels passes through private property over which park officials have no control. They would like to expand the National Monument from 800 to 6,000 acres, but a freeze on new federal land purchases rules this out. Several private non-profit organizations are attempting to raise the $4 to $5 million necessary to consolidate ownership of this piece of American heritage.

Above: *Custer Battlefield, with markers where Custer's men made their last stand.* — John Alwin

Left: *Sitting Bull, although he did not fight at the massacre in June, 1876, was the spiritual leader of the Sioux war.* — Courtesy, Montana Historical Society

Right: *Wooden Leg, Cheyenne, did indeed fight and is much revered by Northern Cheyenne.* — Courtesy, Montana Historical Society

Left: *Glory days on the open range. Circle Diamond cattle near Hinsdale.* — Courtesy, Montana Historical Society

Beginning in the 1870s, cattlemen began to spill out of western Montana valleys and onto the lush prairies of central Montana, especially the fertile Judith Basin country.

Initially the federal government granted tribes gigantic reservations. But as the white settlement frontier approached and eventually engulfed the region, farmers and stockmen, rail and town promoters and others in the vanguard of white settlers clamored for these reserves. They coveted the sprawling Indian lands on which they envisioned seemingly unlimited grazing, a patchwork of prosperous farms, and a network of towns and villages tied together by rail and road. In short, they wanted these lands opened for progress. Pressures mounted and by treaty and executive agreements reservations were whittled down.

With potentially hostile Indians confined to progressively smaller reserves and under the watchful eyes of garrisons of soldiers, white man's use and occupancy of the plains increased. Some of the earliest white settlers were

cattlemen who were lured into the area by the grassy expanses that once supported millions of bison.

Beginning in the 1870s cattlemen began to spill out of western Montana valleys and onto the lush prairies of central Montana, especially the fertile Judith Basin country. Beginning in 1880 nearby Fort Maginnis provided added security for this region. In 1877 Fort Custer was built near the site of the former battle and Fort Keogh was erected at the juncture of the Yellowstone and Tongue rivers. These later two posts helped secure this rich lower Yellowstone region for cattlemen who soon funneled into the valley.

These recently vacated Indian lands were public domain, unfenced and free for the using. Initially, established ranchers and other well-heeled businessmen from the western valleys tested and proved the commercial potential for these eastern grasslands. But by the early 1880s get-rich-quick investors from the eastern United States and Europe were drawn to speculation in the industry by boomer literature like James Brisbin's 1881 classic, *The Beef Bonanza, or How to Get Rich on the Plains.*

The rush was on to cash in. Many a Hollywood movie has immortalized this romantic cowboy era of cattle barons, rustlers and horse thieves, gunslinging

cowhands and vigilantes. Eastern Montana had them all.

One of the most noted aspects of the range livestock industry was the long cattle drives that brought herds northward from as far south as the overstocked ranges of Texas. Like other cattle on the Eastern Montana plains, these were fed and fattened on the region's highly regarded range and then driven to railheads outside Montana for shipment to market, especially in the eastern United States and Europe.

Much has been written about the disastrous winter of 1886-87 and its impact on the range cattle industry. Losses were staggering in some sections of Eastern Montana and more than one historian has suggested that The Hard Winter of '86-'87 put an end to the range cattle industry. This was not the case. Rather than disappearing in a season, the industry only gradually yielded to farmers' fences. Sections of eastcentral Montana remained open range until the early 20th century. Homesteaders still can be found who recall the reluctance with which these cattlemen stepped aside for them when they first fenced their land as recently as the middle Teens.

Clockwise from Above: *Cowboy camp, North Fork of the Milk River, 1894; Cowboy Postcard; Cowboy Crew near Big Sandy 1890s.* — Courtesy, Montana Historical Society

Courtesy Pinkerton's Inc.

KID CURRY

The most dangerous man in America's Wild West was noted western historian James D. Horan's assessment of Kid Curry after more than three decades of researching gunfighters the likes of Billy the Kid, Butch Cassidy and Jesse James. This infamous killer, outlaw, rustler and fugitive had a close tie to Eastern Montana.

In 1884 Kid Curry, then in his teens, and one of his brothers traveled west from Missouri, lured by the romance of cowboy life. They settled in the Little Rockies area and hired on as riders for the Circle C outfit. At this time both still went by their legal name of Logan. History was to remember Harry "Kid" Logan under his alias of Kid Curry.

Before long the brothers pooled their money with another Circle C cowboy and bought a ranch about six miles south of Landusky. They became members of the community, frequenting the local establishments in Landusky and Zortman and driving their cattle to the Great Northern railheads of Malta, Chinook and Harlem, just like other area ranchers. Hank left and was replaced by two other Logans who joined brother Harry raising horses and cattle. This was evidently about when the brothers assumed the name Curry. Why, nobody knows for sure. For Kid Curry this rather conventional life on the western frontier changed abruptly in the winter of 1894.

On December 27, a simmering feud between the Kid and Powell "Pike" Landusky, for whom the town was named, came to a boil. In Jew Jake's saloon, a fisticuffs ended with the Kid fatally shooting Pike with two shots from his single-action Colt 45. Kid Curry might have been able to plead self defense in court, but he didn't wait to find out. When a murder warrant for his arrest was issued, he fled and embarked upon his legendary life of crime.

Initial reports showed he moved south to Wyoming where he began riding with Flat Nose George Currie's gang of horse thieves and rustlers. From a base in the Powder River country they wreaked havoc among cattle and sheep ranchers in a territory including Nevada, Utah, Montana, Wyoming and South Dakota.

Kid Curry and the gang graduated to bank robbing in June 1897, when they held up the Butte County Bank in Belle Fourche, South Dakota. Curry had a hideout in his old stomping grounds, lost in the maze of badlands south of the Little Rockies, and this may have been where the gang headed after their South Dakota bank heist. A posse chased them into Montana and finally cornered and captured the group in Fergus County. Curry and his bunch were shipped off to jail in Deadwood, South Dakota, but escaped in just a matter of weeks.

It didn't take long before the gang was again back in business. On June 2, 1899 they held up the Union Pacific's Overland Flyer west of Cheyenne. By the 19th of June an $18,000 reward had been issued for the gang members — dead or alive. Hotly pursued by several posses, the gang killed one sheriff in an ambush. The next month witnesses identifed the Kid as a participant in the robbery of the Colorado and Southern train at Folsom, New Mexico.

After Flat Nose George Currie was killed in a shoot out with a Utah posse in 1900, Kid Curry took over as the gang's undisputed leader. Within a year they merged with the equally notorious Butch Cassidy's Wild Bunch, forming one of the most awesome assemblages of outlaws the West had ever known.

Almost immediately the newly constituted Wild Bunch struck in a daring train robbery along Montana's Hi-Line. In early July 1901, Kid Curry, along with Butch Cassidy, the Sundance Kid and two other gang members, held up a Great Northern train near Wagner, Montana, just west of Malta. Using dynamite they blew off the front of the express car safe and also succeeded in blowing off part of the roof and side of the car. Before fleeing the area, Kid evidently returned briefly to the Little Rockies country to kill the man who had taken his brother's life five years earlier.

Living comfortably on the booty of his train and bank robberies, Kid Curry drifted toward the warmer climes of the southeast, stopping in Knoxville, Tennessee before the end of the year. There an argument in a saloon ended with the Kid shooting two men and eventually being arrested and jailed. While incarcerated, this living legend became the biggest show in town. The local sheriff declared an open house and thousands of Knoxville's citizens lined up to see and chat with this folk hero. A local paper even referred to him as the "Napoleon of Crime."

By the next winter Curry had been tried and given a long jail sentence and a fine of several thousand dollars. His appeal was unsuccessful and he was awaiting transfer to a federal penitentiary in June 1903, when he again managed an ingenious escape.

No one knows for sure where the Kid next headed, although there was a suggestion that he returned to Montana's Little Rockies. In 1904 the *Great Falls Tribune* reported that he had been identified in Denver, Colorado. Later that year three desperados held up a train in that state. A posse trailed them and wounded one Tap Duncan, who took his own life rather than be captured. The next month Duncan's body was exhumed from its Glenwood Springs grave at the request of the Pinkerton Detective Agency and identified as the body of Kid Curry. The identification was questioned, but the Pinkerton Agency was convinced. Finally, after years of pursuit, they placed Kid Curry in their "Dead and Inactive" file.

Those who reject this identification have their own ideas on what became of the Kid after escaping from his Knoxville cell. One story has him moving to South America and periodically visiting this country incognito. Another reports that he returned to a life of crime in Wyoming.

In research for his 1976 article on Kid Curry, Robert E. Miller uncovered some intriguing references to the Kid. In 1962 Sheriff Dave Middlemas of Helena was told of a man seen in Visalia, California, who was believed to be the Kid. Investigation proved this to be a false lead. Then in 1972, a researcher with the Alaska Department of Public Safety wrote to Montana for particulars on the Kid when distinguishing marks on the body of a recently deceased old prospector aroused his curiosity.

One consequence of the harsh winter of 1886-87 was an expansion of Montana's sheep industry. Sheep had fared better than cattle during that winter and between 1886 and 1900 their numbers increased by about eight-fold to more than 6,000,000.

The range cattle industry did not promote a dense network of towns. In fact, the cattlemen thrived on wide open spaces devoid of people and competition for land use. During the 1880s the appearance of a new element in the geography of Eastern Montana more than any other factor assured the eventual end of the range cattle industry. This new element was the railroad.

The decade of the 1880s witnessed nothing less than a transportation revolution in Eastern Montana. The Northern Pacific Railroad completed its line across the southern tier in the first half of the '80s and the Great Northern spanned most of Montana's plains along a more northerly route by the second half of the decade. Branch lines and other railroads followed.

Initially, newly appearing rail towns like Miles City and Malta functioned primarily as cow towns, serving many of the same functions of once more distant shipping points. But ready access to railroad transportation within Eastern Montana also meant that other agricultural products could be shipped to market. It was no longer a prerequisite that agricultural commodities be able to walk themselves at least part way to market. Almost overnight, cropping production for export beyond a local market became a viable proposition.

Nov. 1916, grain wagons at the Big Sandy elevators.–Courtesy, Montana Historical Society

Fertile river valleys were the first to pass to the new agrarian land owners. These often more fertile and better watered lands, such as along the Yellowstone and Milk River valleys, had the added advantage of immediate access to rail service. It was along these linear belts that many of the plains' earliest towns developed, within what became in 1889 the eastern section of the new state of Montana.

Widespread occupancy of Eastern Montana did not begin, however, until after the turn of the century. Then several significant factors combined to stimulate a population explosion. Expansion of the regional railnet, promotional campaigns by rail carriers, favorable weather, more liberal homestead laws, dearth of other extensive homesteading areas and good markets were some of the factors that contributed to a rush of homesteaders into Eastern Montana during the early 1900s.

The annual number and combined acreages of homestead entries held relatively constant during most of the first decade of the new century and then accelerated to a peak in 1917 and 1918. In 1919 dry weather struck areas of Eastern Montana and the number of homestead entries plummeted. The euphoria that had accompanied the rapid increase in population, business activity, wheat prices and land values during most of the Teens was not to be repeated in the following

decade. As so often has happened in the drier sections of the Great Plains, a bust was again to follow a boom. Rather than continued growth, many Eastern Montana counties experienced a period of population contraction and agricultural readjustment. Drier years, insect pests, lower yields, depressed prices and heavy farm indebtedness forced many farmers out of business and out of the region. Literally tens of thousands left their homesteads behind.

The dry Depression decade of the 1930s witnessed a continued thinning of rural populace in many areas. Today, older residents pensively recall what became almost a wholesale abandonment of some farming areas. Many older residents recollect the late Teens when there seemed to be a family on almost every half section, and four or five neighbors might be seen from a farmhouse window. In the '30s they watched settlement thin when up to half a county's farmers might have folded. By the thousands once hopeful farmers simultaneously were pushed off the land and out of the region by impossible weather and economics, and were pulled away by the hope of jobs both near and far. Most who left never returned.

Those who remained behind were usually the persistent ones. Perhaps it was their stubbornness, their strength or maybe their love of this land that allowed them to weather the bad times. These proud people and their descendants constitute the nucleus of what is Eastern Montana today.

Left: *Via Cooper, 1920, and,* Right: *in 1981 in front of her Brusett area homestead.*

John Alwin

ALMA "VIA" COOPER

On a cold spring day in March 1919, 24-year-old Alma "Via" Cooper stepped off the Northern Pacific train at Miles City. She had traveled west from Dodge City, Kansas, on her own, since her husband had preceded her to Montana and their new Garfield County home. After a three-day wait at Miles City, she joined other homesteaders taking Howard Reeves' touring-car service into Jordan, some 90 miles to the northwest.

Today a drive between Miles City and Jordan is a quick, one-and-a-half-hour trip over a paved highway, and Jordan residents think nothing of driving into Miles for an evening show and returning the same night. But in 1919 it could be a tedious, several-day expedition over ungraded prairie trails. Via and her party spent their first night at what travelers called Halfway House, a private home about midway between Miles City and Jordan. The second night on the road they boarded at the Brackett ranch, and the next morning proceeded in a horse-drawn Indian Wagon, behind a small pung, or sled, that cleared the way through the snow. Jordan was finally reached around noon on the third day!

Via continued by sled to her homestead northwest of Brusett, in the Blackfoot area of the county's northwestern corner. Even though she would be living less than 40 miles from the county seat of Jordan, she would not again visit that community for four years.

Via's husband had come west several years earlier in an immigrant railroad car that carried him, his brother and his father-in-law from Kansas to Wyoming. From Wyoming they headed north to Montana with two wagons, two mares, eight mules, a cook stove and a breaking plow. That first winter the three men lived in a dugout carved into the slope of a hill. By the time Via arrived, her husband already had filed on their 320-acre homestead and built a solid 12'x14' cabin using lumber from the nearby forested Breaks. Her new home had a native lumber floor, and a tar-

paper roof covered with clinker. For years their sole source of heat was a cooking stove, fueled by coal they dug from a small mine in the Breaks also worked by several other local families. An addition was built later, but this would be Via's home until 1944.

Like many beginning homesteaders they were mixed farmers, raising both crops and livestock. The first spring, Via remembers the several-day trip 80 miles south to the Milwaukee Railroad shipping point of Ingomar with two wagons loaded with grain and pulled in tandem by six horses. They soon began shifting emphasis to livestock, and such outings became rare for Via since women did not participate in cattle drives to the railhead.

Work filled most of Via's days, but there was also time for recreation. At first they could not afford to subscribe to the weekly Jordan newspaper, but within a few years Via was enjoying two magazine subscriptions. She and a neighbor each subscribed to a magazine they shared with the other — *Woman's Home Companion* and *Ladies' Home Journal*.

Via and her husband were successful farmers — in 1929 they purchased a used 1927 Chevrolet. Roads at the time were poor by today's standards and often were impassable after rains when, as Via reluctantly relates, "they were as slippery as snot on a door knob." Around 1930 they obtained a battery system to run their lights and radio and kept it charged with a two-blade windmill-like tower. In 1935 they were able to build an addition to their original structure.

Today the weather-checked homestead sits abandoned next to a newer and larger farmhouse occupied by Via's son, Glenn. He and his two sons now operate the homestead, which has grown to a highly mechanized 6,200-acre mixed farming operation.

PART III

EASTERN MONTANA THE PEOPLE, NEIGHBORHOOD BY NEIGHBORHOOD

This place, Eastern Montana, is immense. Its 100,000 square miles is greater than all but seven of the other 49 states. it is larger than West Germany or the United Kingdom. Denmark, Belgium, the Netherlands, Switzerland and Ireland combined could all fit within its borders with thousands of square miles to spare.

Big size means long distances. The 600-mile drive from Alzada in the southeast to Browning in the northwest is greater than the mileage between Billings and Denver, Colorado, or from Portland, Maine to Arlington, Virginia. Long distances permeate many aspects of life in the region, but residents seem to take them in stride. To compete against their league rivals, coach and players on the Wibaux High Longhorns basketball team, as well as loyal fans, must regularly travel one-way distances ranging from a relatively close 58 miles to play Plevna, to as far as the 225-mile expedition to take on the Busby Eagles. On occasion Eastern Montanans may curse such long trips or the necessity of having to drive two hours merely to get into town, but almost always apparent is a deep-seated pride in the spaciousness of their land and their ability to cope with it.

Along with Eastern Montana's large size and long distances is a remarkable sparcity of population. Even though the region includes the state's two largest communities of Billings and Great Falls, and population density does vary, the area is thinly populated by almost any standard. If its approximately 400,000 residents were spread out evenly across the region there would be but four people per square mile. By comparison, Rhode Island has a density of just over 800 people per square mile, New Jersey's density is approaching the 1,000 mark, and the District of Columbia (D.C.) already has over 10,000 people for every square mile. Few areas of comparable size in the United States, outside of Alaska, afford more elbowroom to its residents than does Eastern Montana.

In many sections of our nation the natural landscape has been virtually obliterated by man. His carefully surveyed agricultural fields superimpose a patchwork quilt design over the land, his dense mesh of railroads and power lines crisscross the landscape connecting closely spaced communities in an urban network which ranges upward to large and sprawling metropolitan areas. In such places man and his works dominate, and the landscape has a tamed appearance, manicured and mastered so that much of the original look of the land is lost.

Despite the fact that it has been inhabited for at least 12,000 years and more than 90 percent of the land area is now used for some form of agriculture, Eastern Montana retains a rawness and a naturalness that defy its long-term occupance. There are sections around urban centers and within more productive cropping areas where man's imprint pervades, but these are the exceptions. More common

> Eastern Montana is larger than West Germany or the United Kingdom. Denmark, Belgium, the Netherlands, Switzerland and Ireland combined could fit within its borders.

is a semiarid rangeland setting in which signs of scattered human occupation are quickly engulfed by the spaciousness of the encompassing and largely unworked landscape.

Large-scale white settlement here was relatively recent and visual reminders from pioneer days are a common site. Most area towns still have false front downtown buildings which date from their infancy, and rural areas are dotted with the abandoned and decaying ranch and farm buildings of the region's first agriculturalists.

To outsiders from long settled portions of the United States or foreign countries, this is a source of fascination. In his insightful article entitled "A Montana Journal," which appeared in a recent issue of Northwest Orient Airlines' *Passages*, British correspondent Christopher Portway wrote "Although I come from a country of a much older history, I find that of a more recent past easier to grasp and identify with since it is not yet entirely divorced from present-day reality." Perhaps this is why visitors to Eastern Montana invariably leave bedecked in traditional western dress, or at the least, sporting a cowboy hat. How many tourists visiting the New England states return home in colonial garb?

To say that today's Eastern Montana is a big, semiarid place, which is sparsely populated and dominately agricultural, largely untamed, and relatively young helps explain the general personality and character of this land and its people. But to really know them requires a closer inspection. To help accomplish this, Eastern Montana will be subdivided into six component regions: 1) Triangle, 2) Mid Hi-Line, 3) Northeast, 4) Big Open, 5) Central, and 6) Yellowstone Country.

Geographers are always dividing places into component regions. A place the size of Eastern Montana is too unwieldy to deal with as a single unit, and dividing it into parts produces subregions better suited for a closer look. Any geographical region should have at least one shared trait, and each of our six regions does. But that does not mean Eastern Montana cannot be broken into other equally valid regions. Ours, like most all geographical regions, should be thought of as having transitional borders, the boundary lines being merely approximations.

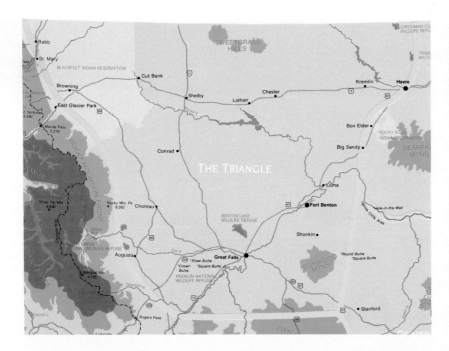

THE TRIANGLE

If you draw a line connecting Great Falls, Havre, Cut Bank, and back to Great Falls, you will have approximated the limits of Montana's internationally renowned "Golden Triangle." This is a classic example of a geographer's perceptual, or vernacular region. State highway maps do not locate or identify it, nor do roadside markers announce when you enter or leave. This is a region perceived to exist by its residents and those of the state, not because of official designation and delimitation, but because people sense it has an identity of its own and shared features that set it apart from surrounding areas. Its reality is reflected in the widespread acceptance and use of the regional name, even by some local businesses.

The Golden Triangle is the premier dryland grain farming area in the state.

The Golden Triangle is the premier dryland grain farming area in the state. Mere mention of the term to most Montanans conjures up images of subdued landscapes veneered in seemingly endless striped grain fields, and a place where towering grain elevators rise from the railroad sidings of even the smallest of towns.

In everyday usage this most productive and prosperous of Montana's non-irrigated farming areas is usually simply referred to as the Triangle. That term has been borrowed here and applied to a somewhat larger area. Included is a belt of surrounding territory in which cash grain farming varies in importance. In this peripheral area factors such as rougher topography, poorer soil, and competition with irrigated agriculture limit dryland grain farming.

The core area, the Golden Triangle, has nearly ideal conditions for dryland wheat production. Soils tend to be fertile and well drained. And since the area was glaciated during the last Ice Age, topography is generally flat to gently rolling, thereby facilitating the operation of the machinery so essential to this highly mechanized type of farming. As in most all of Montana, precipitation is concentrated during the critical spring growing season, just when young plants need it most.

Older economic geography textbooks show the area as part of a large international spring wheat region that spills south out of Canada. But as area residents know, winter wheat ranks number one and huge production in this area helps make it Montana's dominant crop. Winter wheat is planted in late summer or fall, germinates, and sends small shoots up before cold sets in. During winter the young plants lie dormant, but with the first warm weather of spring, renew their growth.

Opposite Page: *Round barn in the Knees Hills, Conrad area.* — R. C. Dommer

Top: *Fruits of the Harvest. Grain in excess of storage at Lothair.* — John Alwin

Bottom: *On-farm grain storage. Kenneth Flynn ranch outside Kremlin.* — John Alwin

In many sections of the North American Great Plains, winters are too severe for young wheat plants to survive, so emphasis is on spring wheat, which is planted in the spring and harvested in late summer or early fall. But more hardy varieties of winter wheat coupled with some unique climatic qualities in northcentral Montana's Triangle allow winter wheat to thrive. Tucked up in the northwestern corner of Great Plains Montana this region is far enough west and high enough in terms of elevation to be spared some of the sub-zero winter temperatures that move south out of Canada and blanket topographically lower areas further east. Additionally, a protective covering of snow is usually present which helps insulate plants from extremely low and potentially killing winter temperatures.

Although winter wheat is king, area counties also produce much of the state's barley and up to half its spring wheat. Each year neighboring Hill and Choteau counties vie for title of Montana's most productive county based on cash receipts from crops. In recent years, harvested wheat acreage alone in each has totaled about one-half million acres.

> Each year neighboring Hill and Choteau counties vie for the title of Montana's most productive county in terms of cash receipts from crops.

Like other dryland farming areas in Eastern Montana this region experienced oversettlement during the early years of the century. And like other sections of Great Plains Montana, it also suffered through the difficult years of large-scale exodus in the 1920s and 1930s. But unlike many other quarters, it was able to retain a more dense rural populace owing to the greater productivity of the land. Today, even though it is far from overcrowded, it remains the state's most densely settled rural area of its size.

As in other of Montana's non-irrigated areas, the 320-acre, homestead-size farm has long been obsolete. The average size for area cash grain farms is now about 2,200 acres, and that figure increases yearly. Although large, this is smaller than the minimum required acreage in most other non-irrigated farming and ranching areas in Eastern Montana. Most farms in the Triangle region are family owned and operated with the largest exception being the more than twenty Hutterite colonies which average several times the size of surrounding farms.

For its size, the Triangle has the most humanized landscape in Montana. Within the most productive sections of the Golden Triangle it is difficult to find large parcels not visually impacted by man. In such areas, intensity of occupancy is reminiscent of Kansas or other more densely settled plains states than it is typical of Eastern Montana.

During the homesteading era population density was even higher. Pioneering farmers began moving into this region in significant numbers during the early 1900s and the influx swelled to a flood in the 1909-11 peak. These were wet years by comparison with long-term averages, and grain crops thrived. The high natural soil fertility coupled with weed free virgin soil, a lack of insect pests, and high wartime prices motivated farmers to plant as much ground as possible. Optimism and prosperity continued to build until 1917 when a drought struck and continued with little relief until 1920. A back to back series of bad years was too much for many and their farms were foreclosed, their dreams of prosperity on the Montana frontier unrealized. Today, abandoned and weatherworn farmsteads are reminders of those who did not succeed.

Above: *Big Sandy and fields beyond.* — Ken Turner

Below: *ERTS (Earth Resources Technology Satellite) false-color infrared image of the northeastern portion of the Triangle.*

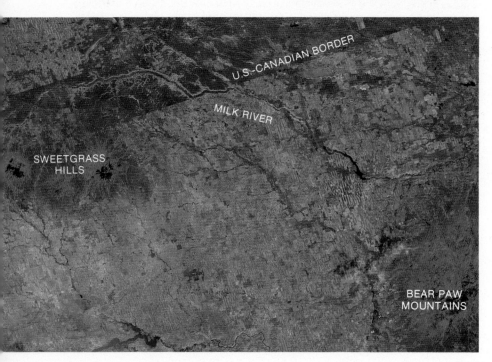

U.S.-CANADIAN BORDER

MILK RIVER

SWEETGRASS HILLS

BEAR PAW MOUNTAINS

Another reminder of the earlier times is the close spacing of communities along railroads within more fertile farming areas. Driving west out of Havre along U.S. 2, one goes through a whole string of these grain collection towns and their railside row of elevators. In a space of only 41 miles, one passes through Kremlin, Gildford, Hingham, Rudyard, Inverness, Joplin, and Chester. This close spacing may have made sense in the era of more dense population and horse-drawn grain wagons, but with a thinning of population and improved transportation it is no longer an economic necessity. Many such small towns are struggling for survival and are now only shadows of their former selves.

> For many small grain-handling towns a shift to grain subterminals and unit trains spells the end of local elevators.

For many small grain-handling towns a shift to grain subterminals and unit trains has some serious implications. Lower multi-car grain hauling rates for 26-car trains and unit trains of 52 cars available at only more widely spaced and much larger capacity subterminals, spell the end for many smaller elevators. In some areas rail abandonments (or "rationalization," depending on one's perspective), especially of branch lines, already have left former railside grain collection points without service.

Block summer fallowing was already an accepted part of "scientific" dryland farming by the early 1900s, although evidently only a minority of Triangle farmers used fallowing prior to the onset of the drought which began in 1917. In an average year on these semiarid plains, moisture isn't always adequate to grow dryland crops in the same field year after year. By leaving land fallow, or unplanted, and cultivating to control weeds during summer, it was found that soil moisture built up and helped assure a better crop. But the initial years had been abnormally wet, and fields produced large yields without fallowing. Farmers fortunate enough to make it through the dry late Teens realized they would have to change their farming practices to better cope with the uncertainty of precipitation in the Triangle area.

Today's cash grain farming areas can be identified easily from the air by the distinctive zebra stripe cropping pattern that has come to characterize dryland grain fields. Montana historian Joseph Kinsey Howard credits Canadians across the border in Alberta with introducing strip farming to Montanans. According to Howard, Alberta farmers began experimenting with alternating cropping systems during the dry years of the late Teens. They narrowed the width of their fallow fields, alternated strips of crops and fallow, and oriented strips at right angles to the prevailing wind to minimize erosion. Word of the technique spread south of the border and Montanans went north to check out its potential. Most liked what they saw and returned home to try out the new field system. Soon strip farming clubs were organized and by 1922 the director of the Montana Agricultural Experiment Station advocated the practice. In the 1930s the Agricultural Adjustment Administration's Montana committee virtually made strip cropping mandatory.

The now widespread practice of summer fallowing is apparently linked to a growing problem in grain areas here and in other dry farming districts of Eastern Montana. The problem is saline seep and it may have affected 250,000 acres of once productive grain land statewide. A saline seep is really just a very slow flowing spring of salty water. Affected areas in grain fields are eventually lost to production when salty soil reaches levels that are toxic to grains. Once well established, saline seeps can almost never be economically reclaimed.

Saline seep on the "north bench" of the Highwood Mountains. — Ken Turner

SALINE SEEP

Before white man moved onto the plains of Eastern Montana nature's vegetative cover had adjusted nicely to the natural environment. Below ground, a dense network of roots reached deep to tap what was periodically sparse soil moisture. Any bare area produced by natural causes was quickly revegetated.

The natural grassland cover is now largely gone from major dryland farming areas in Eastern Montana, replaced by cultivated strips of grain and fallow. Now some of the precipitation that falls percolates into the soil and instead of being intercepted by an intricate root network of natural grasses and shrubs, it merely accumulates below the shallow and sparse overlying root zone. Areas with crop cover use some of this moisture, but fallow areas have no intercepting roots to draw up the water. In areas underlain by an impermeable shale layer (common in Eastern Montana), water accumulates underground, perched above the impenetrable shale zone where it absorbs water-soluable salts. Eventually, just like a sponge, soil and subsoil reach a saturation point and water begins to move downslope along the upper surface of the shale layer.

The trouble comes when the salt-charged underground waters reach the surface. These discharge areas are saline seeps.

The relationship between summer fallow and saline seep is well documented, but still there has not been a rush to abandon the traditional strip-cropping field. Like the rest of us, farmers are creatures of habit and find it hard to abandon what

has been routine for them and for their fathers. The problem is made especially difficult to deal with since recharge areas, where the precipitation soaks into the ground, may be on fallow fields belonging to one farmer, but it's the guy next door who ends up with the saline seep.

There appears to be a number of partial solutions to saline seep in Eastern Montana. The best solution is the one that eliminates the problem before it appears. Less widespread use of summer fallow and greater consideration of a more flexible cropping system seem to have potential. Saline seep experts have suggested that instead of just assuming a fallow period at a regular interval for each parcel of land, grain farmers should not decide until soil moisture conditions are actually tested. Some areas may be able to support more of a continuous cropping.

A less geometric pattern which takes hydro-geologic factors into account and keeps potential recharge areas continuously covered with vegetation might also help stem the formation of new saline seeps. These new approaches to grain farming are now being tested by some innovative Eastern Montana farmers.

At the earliest signs of a seep farmers can sometimes arrest its further development with appropriate action. Artificial underground drainage and land grading in the recharge area can help. Sowing deep-rooted plants in a recharge area tends to "pump" up excess water. Four-year-old alfalfa can put down 18-foot-deep roots and has proven to be an especially good "pump."

In the western section of the Triangle striped wheat fields give way to blocks of irrigated farmland and much smaller farms. Here two major irrigation projects dominate — the Valier and the Sun River. The former is the older of the two, dating back to the early part of this century. It began as a commercial venture by the industrious Conrad brothers and has remained a privately funded undertaking. Today irrigated acreage in the project totals some 76,000 acres, all within Pondera County. Irrigated hay and pasture used to be the dominant land use, but now in a typical year about 40% of the acreage is in barley, 30% in wheat (winter and spring), 20% hay and the remaining 10% other crops and pasture. Barley yields of from 75 to 85 bushels per acre and wheat yields of 60 to 65 bushels per acre are commonplace, about double the yields on adjacent dryland farms.

To the south, west of Great Falls, is the newer and even larger Sun River Irrigation Project developed by the United States Bureau of Reclamation between 1914 and 1920. Gibson, Pishkun and Willow Creek reservoirs hold back sufficient water to irrigate a total of 92,000 acres within the project's two districts. As with the Valier project, high productivity of irrigated land is reflected in much smaller farm size. An average-size farm in the Greenfield District now covers about 270 acres. Farmers experimented with different types of row crops (sugar beets, beans, and silage corn) until the 1960s, but abandoned those crops because of climatic limitations, inadequate water supply, and problems with access to processing plants. Now barley and wheat account for about 65% of the acreage, hay another 20% and pasture the remaining 15%.

Although the Triangle has long been a land of farms and ranches, and agriculture has held sway for generations, energy production also has a long history. The first fuel exploited was coal, mined commercially from the Great Falls Field beginning in the 1870s. Coal mining fostered the development of towns such as Belt, Stockett, Tracy, and Sand Coulee, and others that are now ghost towns in the hill country in this distinctive southeastern corner of the region.

Top: *High in the Highwood Mountains.* — Mark Thompson

Bottom Left: *Polled Hereford ranch east of Pendroy.* — John Alwin

Bottom Right: *Rock City north of Valier.* — Rick Graetz

Above: *The Free Ferry across the Missouri near Loma, and* Right: *its operators, Ray and Pam Scheele. They average 900 to 1,000 crossings per month on the 35-year-old vessel operated by a tractor motor.* — John Alwin photos

Below: *The Galata Community Hall.* — John Alwin

With the development of Great Falls and the arrival of the Great Northern Railroad in the 1880s, demand for coal skyrocketed and thousands of miners, including Poles, Italians, Slavs, and Finns immigrated to newly founded towns.

With the development of Great Falls and the arrival of the Great Northern Railroad in the 1880s, demand for this coal skyrocketed. New mines were opened and literally thousands of miners, including hundreds of Poles, Italians, Slavs, and Finns immigrated to newly founded towns. By the 1890s the Great Northern relied on this coal to fuel its steam locomotives for hundreds of miles in both directions along its line. Additional coal was used at huge copper smelting and refining operations in Great Falls. By the 1890s Cascade County led the state in coal production, and in 1900 Belt and Stockett had several times their present populations.

Beginning in the 1920s area coal production and associated population dropped dramatically. Natural gas began replacing coal as a fuel in the consumptive ore smelting/refining process as well as in domestic use, and the Great Northern began to replace its coal-fired locomotives with newer oil-burning engines. One by one the mines closed. Today abandoned mines and coke ovens and the colorful ethnic mix of population are reminders of these former boom days.

While the energy picture dimmed in the hill country in the southeast, oil and gas discoveries led to an energy boom of a different sort in the north. In 1922 oil was discovered in what proved to be the rich and extensive Kevin-Sunburst Field, just south of the Canadian line. During the '20s it dominated Montana's still-young petroleum industry. For several years it was the state's first ranked field and in its peak year of 1926 accounted for almost 85 percent of state petroleum production.

The decade of the 1930s saw first wildcatting, and soon number one state ranking, shift to the new Cut Bank Field. Discovered in 1931, production increased there while that of the neighboring Kevin-Sunburst Field declined. Rapid development of the Cut Bank Field was linked to its higher grade oil and wealthy corporations, including the Montana Power Company, which owned huge acreages. In 1936 the Cut Bank Field climbed to the state's number one position, a title it could claim until the 1950s when large discoveries were made further east near the Montana-North Dakota border.

Both these north Triangle fields, as well as several others, are still producing, although they now account for less than 20 percent of state petroleum production. The hunt for new energy in the region has shifted to the west into the rolling foothills off the east flank of the Rockies, an area associated with the geologic province known as the "Disturbed Belt" or "Overthrust Belt." Here, rocks now on this east side of the Rockies once may have been on the other, west side of the Divide. Massive tectonic forces have thrust sheets of these sedimentary rocks eastward and in the process, created geologic structures that favor the accumulation of oil and gas. This same zone has produced huge finds to the north in Alberta and to the south in Wyoming. Discoveries already have been made and more are expected. West of our region and still within the Overthrust Belt, the hunt for oil and gas is now hotly debated. Energy companies are eager to tap the region, but others question the appropriateness of large scale exploration/exploitation in the pristine Bob Marshall and adjacent wilderness areas. Although outside of our Triangle region, activity in the area does have implications for nearby plains towns.

FORT BENTON

Fort Benton has been called the "birthplace of Montana," a reflection of its relatively long and distinguished history. Begun as an American Fur Company trading post in 1847, this proved to be the only Montana fur trading establishment to make the transition to modern town. Its success can be attributed to its strategic location at the head of steamship navigation on the Missouri. The 1860 arrival of the steamboat "Chippewa" ushered in a new commercial phase for the community which would witness its rise to the status of distribution center for much of Montana and an adjacent section of Canada.

The distinctive banks of the Missouri rise steeply along this reach of the river, but nature did provide a wide valley floor and a nearly ideal docking waterfront at the site of Fort Benton. Steamship traffic and the volume of cargoes passing over the wharf grew as mining boomed in the western Montana valleys. It all began with the strike at Grasshopper Creek in 1862 where the town of Bannack was born. Colors were struck in other gulches in quick succession and towns like Virginia City, Nevada City, Deer Lodge, and Helena came into being. Gold from these mines had to be shipped to outside markets and supplies and other merchandise had to be shipped in. Fort Benton quickly assumed the role of entrepôt for these communities.

It was a classic example of a break-in-bulk-point, a place where cargoes had to be unloaded from one mode of carrier and reloaded on another. Cargoes, for example, coming upriver by boat and destined for Western Montana had to be off-loaded from watercraft and loaded into freight wagons to complete their journey. Many a fine piece of furniture still in some of the state's older homes came up the river and passed over the Fort Benton dock, as did thousands of travelers moving to and from the gold fields. All this activity meant jobs for dock workers, warehousemen, freighters and the complement of people necessary to provide the essential goods and services (food stores, clothing stores, banks, dentists, doctors, etc.). This was a natural place for development of a town.

By 1880 Fort Benton's population had grown to 1,618, and it was one of the largest towns in the Montana Territory. The next year construction was begun on the three-story Grand Union Hotel, an inn befitting a community of this stature. When completed in 1882 it boasted the plushest accommodations available between Minneapolis and Seattle.

The old Grand Union remains near the waterfront, and still operates as a hotel. The once bustling levee it faces is now stripped of all evidence of its former commercial role. In its place is an attractive grassy area for strollers and picnickers, with markers to tell visitors of its historic past.

Opposite Page: *Fort Benton,* **Inset:** *Lewis and Clark Expedition Monument with Sacajawea.* — John Alwin, R. C. Dommer

Above: *The Grand Union Hotel at Fort Benton, once the plushest lodging between Seattle and Minneapolis.* — John Alwin

The arrival of railroads in the decade of the 1880s meant an end to Fort Benton's near monopoly on handling cargoes. In 1880 the Utah and Northern Railroad reached Butte, by 1883 the Northern Pacific spanned the entire territory across the south, and in 1887 Hill built his line right through Fort Benton. Railroads were able to offer faster and cheaper service than was possible from a river boat: freight wagon combination, and traffic was quickly diverted to this new mode of transport. The impact was immediate, and by 1890 Fort Benton had lost almost 1,000 of its 1,600 residents.

With its river trade behind it, Fort Benton developed as service and trade center for the surrounding agriculturalists — first for cowboys and cattle barons of the range cattle industry, and with the subsequent influx of homesteaders, for both irrigators and dryland farmers. As county seat for Choteau County the town oversees one of the most prosperous agricultural counties in the state.

Fort Benton is now a popular embarkation point for float trips down the Missouri. Today rubber rafts are launched where steamboats once docked. Next door at the old Grand Union, tourists sleep in the same rooms which once accommodated wealthy shipping magnates and railroad V.I.P.'s. Despite the century of change, enough of the elements remain so that, with a little imagination, one can visualize Fort Benton in its heyday.

GREAT FALLS

The view of Great Falls from along the access road to its international airport atop Gore Hill may be the most encompassing of Montana's second largest community. Behind you, in the distance, some 60 miles to the west, rise the ramparts of the Northern Rockies, and laid out before you the verdant urbanized area of over 70,000 spreads along the banks of the Sun and Missouri as it swings to the east.

This panorama would no doubt please, but probably not surprise Paris Gibson, the man known as the "Father of Great Falls." In the late 1870s he came west from St. Anthony, Minnesota (today's Minneapolis) to begin anew on the Montana frontier. Initially, he settled in the commercial center of Fort Benton, but by the next year had traveled upriver to check out the Great Falls of the Missouri he had read about in the journals of Lewis and Clark.

Paris Gibson knew well the power-generating potential of waterfalls. Back home in St. Anthony he had been a partner in the community's first successful flour mill which used energy from St. Anthony Falls on the Mississippi. Although Gibson most certainly appreciated the beauty of the thundering series of Missouri cascades, it was more their economic potential than their scenic value which lured him.

Gibson quickly became well established in the livestock industry, knew the land, and must have sensed the agricultural potential of this fertile section of the Montana prairie. In the summer of 1882 he returned to the Missouri and selected a site for a newly planned town at the junction of the Sun and Missouri — strategically situated to tap what would surely become a rich agricultural hinterland once a railroad linked the area to outside markets.

Back in the Twin Cities, Gibson had been a pillar of the business and civic community and had made the acquaintance of railroad entrepreneur James J. Hill. In 1879 Hill initiated plans for a transcontinental railroad, the St. Paul, Minneapolis and Manitoba, that was projected to traverse northern Montana. Gibson contacted Hill about plans for a town near Black Eagle Falls and with little difficulty convinced the railroad magnate to join in the venture, although Hill rejected the suggestion that the new community be called "Hillton" in his honor.

With the arrival of Hill's railroad still years away, Gibson set about acquiring the necessary land for the townsite and platting what would become today's north-south and east-west grid of streets and avenues. Unlike many other Eastern Montana towns, Great Falls was a carefully planned community from the start.

Gibson had very definite ideas on how a city should be laid out. One aspect high on his list was wide streets, maybe because he had watched the new town of St. Paul, Minnesota, grow up around its central section of congested narrow avenues. Great Falls was going to be different.

He must have liked the simple layout of streets back in St. Anthony, because he duplicated that pattern on the banks of the Missouri. The main spine of the Great Falls street system is Central Avenue, which runs perpendicular to the shore of the river, the same relationship between St. Anthony's Central Avenue and the Mississippi River. Consecutively numbered "avenues" parallel Central to the north and south both in Great Falls and St. Anthony. A series of numbered "streets" begins at the rivers and continues in sequence in an easterly direction away from the river. The end product is a straightforward grid in which any address conveys a

readily located city block. It is only in more recent additions to Great Falls that this pattern has been abandoned.

Residents and visitors who marvel at the community's abundant mature trees, which the local chamber of commerce tallies at 25,000, can thank Mr. Gibson for his arboreal penchant. He felt a town should be well treed both in its numerous parks and along streets and avenues. As the community's first mayor, Paris Gibson oversaw the municipal planting of literally thousands of ash and elm, many of which are now towering trees almost a century old. Today the city's tree-lined residential streets help give Great Falls more of a Midwestern look than any other Montana town.

On October 15, 1887, Hill's St. Paul, Minneapolis, and Manitoba crew built into Great Falls, having laid parallel ribbons of steel from the North Dakota border to that point in less than six months. Gibson and other eager citizens didn't wait for its arrival before establishing some of the essentials for their prospective boom town. In 1884 Gibson built the community's first flour mill named after St. Anthony's first mill which he had started some two decades earlier. The first schoolhouse was completed in 1885, and the same year the *Great Falls Tribune* began publishing.

The 1890 Census showed Great Falls with a population of almost 4,000, where only ten years earlier the site of the town had but one resident living in a small log cabin on the west side of the Missouri. That year saw the completion of the first dam at Black Eagle Falls. Readily available and relatively cheap power became the magnet that attracted additional milling operations to the city. Other flour mills began operation, and soon Great Falls also had two metal smelting/refining mills.

By the '90s the world was going electrical and Montana's mines at Butte accounted for more than half the United States' copper production and fully a quarter of the world's total. Some ore was treated in Butte, but large quantities were also shipped to Great Falls for processing. The "Electric City" was flush with growth, prosperity, and confidence and launched a brief campaign in 1892 for designation as Montana's capital.

The rally for capital city status was unsuccessful, but growth and prosperity continued at a galloping pace. By the turn of the century Great Falls exceeded Helena in size and with a population of almost 15,000 was the state's second largest community, surpassed only by Butte. Its closest rival in Eastern Montana was Billings, which had less than a fourth as many residents.

Left: *The Father of Great Falls, Paris Gibson.* — Great Falls C. of C.

Above: *Great Falls from airport hill.* —John Alwin

Right, Clockwise: *Great Falls' Giant Springs are billed as the largest fresh-water springs in the world issuing 338.8 million gallons of water per day. The beloved Charles M. Russell in bronze, beside his log studio. Ryan Dam.* — Great Falls C. of C., Al Pavik, Montana Power

Modern day Great Falls has changed. Since early in its youth, manufacturing, and specifically, primary metals refining, had held a firm footing in the local economic base. That is no longer the case. A major blow came in 1973 when the Anaconda Company closed its zinc plant, putting an end to almost 1,000 high-paying jobs. Then in September, 1980, Anaconda announced the permanent shutdown of its Great Falls copper refinery and wire mill. This time 550 well paid employees were jobless and the city was without a primary metal industry for the first time in 80 years.

These two major closures were a shock to the community and sent ripple effects through the entire regional economy. In retrospect, it seems amazing that Great Falls lost less than six percent of its population during those lean years, declining from around 60,000 to about 57,000. Metropolitan population dropped by only about a thousand to 80,700.

While the manufacturing aspect of the city's economic base contracted, its role as regional trade and service center to northcentral Montana increased. For people in a 12- to 15-county area, on farms in the prosperous Golden Triangle, and in communities like Havre, Fort Benton, Browning, Shelby and Conrad, Great Falls is the nearest metropolitan center. When they need specialized medical services,

The base came under control of the Strategic Air Command in 1954 when it was assigned a jet fighter wing. That year fighter pilot Colonel Einar Axel Malmstrom was killed in an aircraft accident near Great Falls and the base was renamed in his memory.

A new chapter began in 1961, when the 341st Strategic Missile Wing was activated and the base became the first Minuteman ICBM wing in the country. Malmstrom was to become nerve center for an awesome array of Minuteman missiles that totaled 150 by 1963 and 200 in 1967. There has been an ongoing program to replace missiles with others that are more accurate and more powerful. Aging Minuteman I's have all been replaced and squadrons now have either Minuteman II's or III's. At this time, the Defense Department is considering replacing at least some of these Minutemen with even larger, MX Missiles. The proposal is a controversial one and has aroused strong feelings on both sides of the issue.

Some Great Falls residents are perfectly happy with the somewhat reduced size of their community, while others would like to see it set new growth records. The Great Falls Area Chamber of Commerce has actively promoted the community and has established a separate Economic Growth Council. The Chamber launched a contest for a new city slogan, and Kelly Bolrath came up the winner with "Great Falls, A City for All Reasons." The Chamber's energy committee is now pushing for the identification of the oil and gas region north of the Little Belt Mountains and between the Rockies and Bear Paws as the "Great Falls Basin." They are hoping the name association will concentrate energy developments in Great Falls, just as they feel it has in Williston, North Dakota, the recognized center of the famed Williston Basin.

Local efforts to convince new businesses to locate in the area already have paid off. Recently, the Montana Power Company selected a site just east of Great Falls for its Resource '89 coal-fired power plant. Construction of the 350 MW generating plant is projected to begin in the mid-'80s and should take three to four years. At its peak, construction will mean 1,000 new jobs. When completed the permanent work force may top 150, and additional new jobs in the county would be generated if Montana Power decides to use coal from the nearby fields around Belt and Sand Coulee.

Community pride runs deep in the Electric City. This message was impressed upon the Anaconda Company in early 1982 when they announced plans to demolish the 506-foot smoke stack at their abandoned copper refinery. Since 1908 the towering stack has stood atop Indian Point, dominating the regional skyline. Paris may have the Eiffel Tower and New York City the Empire State Building, but for 74 years, Great Falls has had the "Big Stack." Many residents were saddened by the prospect of losing this landmark and organized the vocal "Save the Stack" committee to fight the demolition.

Even to the casual observer, it is obvious that Great Falls has a maturity that is lacking in other Eastern Montana urban centers. It has been a large town since the turn of the century, a claim that no other Eastern Montana community can make. This maturity is evident in its urban landscape with its block upon block of early twentieth century homes on streets flanked by grand rows of elm and ash, and in its central business district with its substantial brick and stone architecture. Even though Great Falls' economic prospects have been dimmed by several recent major setbacks, no one can deny that the Electric City still has its spark.

want to hear a Waylon Jennings or John Denver concert, have to make major airline connections, or simply feel like going on an all-out shopping spree, they naturally head for Great Falls. Its service role is obvious in employment statistics which show 18,000 people in the metro area employed in retail and wholesale trade, financing, insurance, real estate, and service areas. That figure is now more than fourteen times the number employed in all manufacturing.

Malmstrom Air Force Base is the Great Falls area's largest employer. Today the base provides jobs for 4,500 military and 550 civilian personnel. Manpower at the base peaked in the early 1970s, and since then transfer of some detachments to other bases has reduced both military and civilian employment.

Although Malmstrom is the home of the country's first Minuteman Missile Defense complex, its beginning goes back to the time of less sophisticated weaponry. Great Falls Army Air Base was built in 1942 as a transit base for lend-lease war materials which were shipped via the Alaska Polar route to the Soviet Union. Older city residents remember when droves of B-17s and B-29s touched down at the base enroute to Alaska and, eventually, war duty overseas. American combat crews for B-17 bombers were trained here during the war and later the base was a practice field for pilots who flew C-54 transports in the Berlin Airlift.

MONTANA'S MINUTEMEN

Malmstrom's 200 Minuteman ICBM's are buried in underground silo launchers scattered over 23,000 square miles of the Montana prairie, from the Shelby area on the northwest to Harlowton and Lewistown in the southeast. This entire region met requirements for the system including relatively constant soil structure, deep water table, and an average elevation of 3,500 feet which gives missiles a head start and represents a six percent fuel savings.

Each Minuteman is housed in a steel and concrete silo about 80 feet deep, called a launch facility (LF). It contains the actual launching tube and missile mounted on a spring shock-suspension system, as well as necessary electronics and an energy power source. The launch tube is covered by a 108-ton sliding door.

Each of the four missile squadrons is assigned 50 Minutemen, which are grouped into clusterings of ten. One launch control center (LCC) is assigned to each group of ten missiles and usually is located near the geographical center of their distribution. LCC's are buried capsules of reinforced concrete and steel, some 60 to 90 feet underground. Walls are 4½ feet thick. An eight-ton blast door seals off the top of the access shaft.

Inside, in an insulated room suspended by pneumatic shock absorbers, are the essential launch equipment and the two-man missile combat crew. Each crew spends 24 hours locked in the capsule and the LCC is always manned. These underground command centers can be made completely self-contained in a post-attack situation, but are otherwise serviced by an above ground launch-control support facility.

Both LF's and LCC's are a common sight in northcentral Montana where they often rise in the middle of farmers' fields. Always housed behind locked gates, chain link fences, and barbed wire, these installations have the highest security. Radar-like surveillance systems, alarms on locks, and seismic sensors immediately warn LCC's Security Police of an unauthorized attempted entry.

MINUTEMAN MISSILES

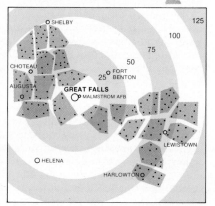

HAVRE

Nestled in the Milk River Valley north of the Bear Paw Mountains is Havre, the northeastern anchor of the Golden Triangle. With a population of 11,000 it is the second-ranking city within the region.

Havre was founded in 1891, and named after Le Havre, France, the birthplace of the two men who originally homesteaded the land on which the town developed. James Hill's St. Paul, Minneapolis and Manitoba Railroad (later the Great Northern) had passed through the site of the future town four years earlier as it swung to the south toward Great Falls. It wasn't until after another line of the newly reorganized Great Northern struck out westward toward the Pacific from this site that there was sufficient impetus for town development at this strategic railroad juncture. From its beginning, the railroad has been the major local employer.

Havre's role as a regional trade center expanded after the turn of the century with an influx of farmers, both in the irrigated Milk River Valley and the nearby dryland areas. In 1912, Hill County was formed and Havre was soon designated county seat. The next year the state acquired 2,000 acres at the former Fort Assiniboine military post ten miles out of town, with the intention of establishing an agricultural and educational center. The Agricultural Experiment Station began operating there in 1915, but it was decided that the site was too far from town for a school. In lieu of that location, the state chose Havre and established Northern Montana College in 1913, although it wasn't until 16 years later that the two-year, vocationally oriented college started up in Havre High School. The present campus was opened in 1932 and in 1954 was designated a four-year college. Programs have expanded and the now more than 1,000 students have a wide range of academic options.

Havre is home to Big Bud Tractors, the manufacturer of the largest production-line, four-wheel-drive tractor in the nation. The company's 30,000-square-foot plant on the west side of Havre produces units ranging up to 650 horsepower. Engines,

axles, and transmissions are brought in from outside, but all other fabrication and assembly is done at the plant. Initially the sprawling wheat fields of the Golden Triangle proved to be a readily available market, but now the tractors are sold worldwide. Units are now in use in Australia, South Africa, Iran, and Canada, as well as other foreign countries and states ranging from Florida to Hawaii.

Above: *Big Bud Tractors, manufactured in Havre, are sold world wide.* — John Alwin

Lower Left: *Havre from the West.* — John Alwin

Lower Right: *Picturesque Cowan Hall on Montana's newest state campus, Northern Montana College.* — John Alwin

Left and Above Left: *A livestock auction in Shelby.* **Above:** *Entertainment agricultural style, a midget tractor pull, Choteau County Fair.* — John Alwin photos

SHELBY

Trivia and boxing devotees recognize this town as the site of the July 4, 1923 world heavyweight championship fight between Jack Dempsey and Tommy Gibbons. The community went all out for the affair. A 40,000-seat hexagonal wooden arena was constructed that was then billed as the world's best boxing facility. Plans were all set with arrangements for special trains to carry the thousands of spectators into Shelby, when a few days before the fight, Dempsey's manager reneged. Trains already had been cancelled by the time he reconsidered. Dempsey won the 15-round fight by decision, but promoters lost more than $100,000. Full paid attendance totaled less than 8,000, but as many as 17,000 gate crashers and reduced-price admissions brought the total crowd to around 25,000.

Like many other communities in the region, Shelby was another railroad spawned town, appearing in 1891 with the arrival of the Great Northern. At first it was a typical cowtown, which local cowboys and sheepmen frequented for supplies and recreation. Homesteaders displaced them after the turn of the century and Shelby developed as a major grain shipment point. The 1922 discovery of the Kevin-Sunburst oil field proved to be an economic stimulus to the town, producing a classic population boom.

Shelby remains one of the largest grain storage centers in northern Montana. One elevator company alone has a capacity of 1,500,000 bushels. Located at the junction of U.S. Highway 2 and Interstate 15, Shelby is also a transportation center and crossroads for the region. North of town the 24-hour border crossing at Coutts-Sweetgrass has the highest traffic count of any crossing between Seattle and Minneapolis. While many Eastern Montana towns its size have been losing population, Shelby has more than held its own. The 1980 Census enumerated over 3,100 residents.

KREMLIN

This little community 20 miles west of Havre is typical of many of the smaller agricultural towns in the Triangle. It developed as homesteaders filled surrounding plains in the early 20th century. By 1916 it boasted three grain elevators, three general stores, two banks, two hotels, saloons, restaurants, lumberyards, hardware stores, and even a new car dealership and newspaper of its own.

Those were the heydays. Today the town's population is less than 200 and its business community has been reduced to two grain elevators, a Cenex station, a garage, one grocery store, an auto body shop and a bar. There is no longer demand for a self-sufficient town since modern transportation means the bright lights of Havre are now only 20 minutes away.

Despite its fall from prominence, Kremlinites are no less proud of their town. There is a strong sense of community, in part fostered by the fact that for better or worse, residents all know each other. Local school children provide much of the entertainment with their sports competition, musicals, and dramas. Once school recesses for the summer, however, regular community social events are more infrequent. Harking back to her high school days in Kremlin, 20-year-old Montana State University student Julie Haugen recalls that "boredom can settle in very quickly." The occasional dance at the bar or school is looked forward to, and is usually attended by both young and old.

Limited local employment opportunities have meant that most young people have had to leave the area following high school graduation. The future is uncertain. Small grain collection points like Kremlin may be severely impacted by the now clear trend to large, regional, grain-collection facilities.

Above: *Blackfeet dancing at Browning.* — Homer Collins

Below: *Remote but not captive, this Kremlin home sports a satellite dish for television reception.* — John Alwin

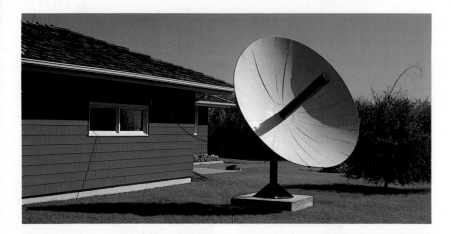

THE BLACKFEET RESERVATION

In area, the 1.5 million acre Blackfeet Indian Reservation is the largest "community" in the Triangle. This scenic Indian nation sprawls eastward onto the plains from its common western border with the mountain splendor of Glacier National Park. From 1855 until 1888 the Blackfeet and neighboring northern Montana tribes roamed a gigantic reservation which encompassed lands north of the Missouri, from the Continental Divide east to the mouth of the Milk River. The Blackfeet were given their own, smaller reservation in the westernmost section of this area in 1888. Their reservation assumed its present configuration eight years later when the tribe ceded what is now the section of Glacier National Park east of the Continental Divide to the federal government in exchange for an annual $150,000 worth of goods and services for a ten-year period.

Of the just over 1.5 million acres within the reservation, about 950,000 are now owned in trust status by individual Indians or by the tribe, and the remaining 38 percent is owned by non-Indians. Almost 70 percent of trust lands is used for grazing, and the remainder is split evenly between forests and cropland, mainly barley, wheat, and hay.

Browning has served as reservation headquarters since 1894 when Old Agency was abandoned in favor of a new site along the just completed Great Northern Railroad. Its 1,200 residents make it the largest town on the reservation. Each year it is the site of rodeos and other festivals, the largest being its North American Indian Days Celebration, held every July at the town's Blackfeet Tribal Fairgrounds. Residents as well as Indians from other reservations pitch their tipis in a wide circle and participate for several days in traditional dancing, singing, drumming, and feasting. Non-Indians are welcome to participate in the celebration.

Browning is also home to the Museum of the Plains Indians. Many visitors enroute to and from Glacier National Park make it a point to stop here to purchase authentic Native American artwork in the associated craft shop. A permanent exhibition gallery illustrates the richness and diversity of historic arts, and the social and ceremonial aspects of eleven plains tribes through dioramas and other displays. The museum's changing exhibition galleries assure repeat visitors something new each time. One especially popular attraction has been a display of painted tipis erected on the museum grounds during summer.

MONTANA'S HUTTERITES

You can see them shopping in Great Falls and Billings, Lewistown, Choteau, and other communities, men dressed in black coats, trousers, and hats, and women in long, brightly colored dresses and head scarves. They are Montana's Hutterites and they are becoming an increasingly more important element in the state's agricultural scene.

The first Hutterites arrived in Montana in 1911, but the group can trace its beginnings to the 16th century and sections of present-day Austria and Czechoslovakia, where the sect was organized during the Protestant Reformation. Like other Anabaptists, which include the Mennonites and Old Order Amish, they rejected infant baptism and membership in a state religion, and were devout pacifists. These beliefs and the insistence on communal ownership and colony life set them even more apart from non-Hutterites. From their founding in 1528 until the late 1780s when they settled in Russia at the invitation of Empress Catherine II, they were repeatedly on the move, searching for a home where they could live free from persecution.

Hutterites again realized it was time to move on in the 1870s when their special educational privileges and exemption from military service were about to be withdrawn. This time they chose the United States for a new home and some 800 Hutterites migrated to South Dakota between 1874 and 1877. About half these new Americans abandoned the communal lifestyle and took up their own homesteads, but the rest organized themselves into three colonies. To this date all Hutterites in North America can trace their lineage back to one of these three colonies, each one of which became the starting point for one of three, somewhat different, Hutterite groups — *Dariusleut*, *Lehrerleut*, and *Schmiedeleut*. Each has its own distinctive discipline and style of dress, and members marry within their particular group.

The Hutterites prospered in South Dakota and added Spring Creek Colony outside Lewistown, Montana, in 1911. Then as so often had happened before, persecution forced them to seek out a new home. This time it was war fever during World War I which whipped up opposition against these German speaking people. In 1918 the Spring Creek Colony closed and its people moved north to Canada, joining all but one American colony in a migration to north of the border.

By the Depression years of the late 1920s and early 1930s, local groups in Montana and the Dakotas sent representatives to Canada to entice Hutterites back to the States. These efficient agriculturalists were able to remain more economically viable than most farmers during these hard times and, all of a sudden, communities realized what an economic asset it would be to have a colony or two in their vicinity. A few were convinced to return, but colonies remained few and far between until the mid-1940s when Alberta began passing legislation limiting the sale of land to Hutterites and setting limits on the size and spacing of colonies. Between 1945 and 1948 Canadian Hutterites established eight colonies in Eastern Montana. By 1970 there were 22 colonies and in 1982 this figure had grown to 37.

For Hutterites, the colony, or *Bruderhof*, is the center of their universe. They view their colony as akin to Noah's Ark and believe that they must reside within it if they are going to receive eternal life. This is their pure and holy cosmos, and the only place they can maintain what Hutterites see as God's order.

MONTAN
HUTTERIT
COLONI

Present 1969
New 1970-1981

Above: *Miller colony.*

Opposite Page and Right: *Scenes from the Martinsdale Colony*

John Alwin photos

Toward evening adults and school-age children use the school house for daily church services. The congregation seats itself according to sex and age, with each person knowing his or her place.

Additional buildings typically associated with this central cluster of structures include small outhouses behind each apartment unit, communal shower and laundry facilities, a food-storage building, and a shoe-making and repair shop. Most other associated buildings reflect the types of farming on the colony. In Montana, this is a commercial, diversified farming which commonly includes cash grain, hogs, eggs and poultry, fresh vegetables, lambs and wool, cattle, and dairy products.

One key function of the *Bruderhof* is to keep members as removed as possible from the outside world. Although they are generally shyly congenial with outsiders and hospitable to guests of the colony, Hutterites view the outside world as a place where sin and temptation can too easily endanger the orderliness of their way of life. Since an average Montana colony controls something like 12,000 acres, physical isolation from neighbors is pretty much assured on a daily basis. Radios and televisions are forbidden on the colony, although there is usually one telephone.

Despite the fact that they shun many aspects of the modern 20th century and continue to make their own clothing, staple foods, soaps, and furniture, and couldn't tell you who the stars are on television, Hutterites incorporate the latest advances in agriculture. Massive four-wheel drive tractors, specialized field equipment and reliance on the best fertilizers, herbicides and insecticides make them some of Montana's most productive farmers.

The Hutterites have to be good farmers since this is their only source of the income necessary for perpetuation of the group. With an extremely high population growth rate, which means a doubling of population about every 18 years (more than four times the national rate), Hutterites have to be able to finance new colonies on a regular basis. Once a colony's population begins to exceed 120 or 130, it is time to divide, half going to a new "daughter" colony and the rest remaining at the "parent" colony. Spacing between parent and daughter colonies varies from hundreds of miles to just a few. The capital outlay necessary to acquire the thousands of agricultural acres and to build and equip a new daughter colony is staggering, and must be borne by the individual parent colony. Once begun, the new colony becomes its own discrete economic unit.

These seem to be times of accelerated change for Montana's Hutterites. Peter Hofer, preacher of the Martinsdale Hutterite Colony west of Harlowton, says that the group is now experiencing more change than any other time in his life. He is concerned that Hutterites are getting away from their traditions. This was really apparent to Peter in the summer of 1981 as their new colony just east of Harlowton was about to start operation. He agreed with incorporating all the latest agricultural advances, such as electronic, computerized milking equipment, but seriously questioned changes like running water and shower facilities in each family apartment. Such change, he feels, has long-term implications for their communal lifestyle.

The Hutterites are an industrious people, who do what they do extremely well. They have managed to maintain their nonconformist lifestyle intact for centuries. And for centuries widespread misconceptions have surrounded this patient group. As Peter Hofer says, "It's nothing new to be misunderstood."

Orderliness permeates all aspects of life in the colony. Most Montana colonies are built on a similar, centuries-old plan. Each building has its proper location and relationship with other structures.

Centrally located is the kitchen-dining hall complex. Like all buildings it always is of a plain and functional style. It is the closest thing there is to a nerve center in the colony. Each day, first school children and then adults assemble there for meals. As with most other activities, ringing of bells announces meal times. Women eat on one side of the dining hall and men on the other, each in the proper seat ranked according to age. Homemade tables are long with benches for seats, floors are spotless and thickly varnished, and walls are without pictures or other adornments.

During the school year children meet for German school for at least an hour both before and after English school, half a day on Saturdays, all public school vacation days, and whenever the English teacher is sick. At these times students practice reading and writing German, and reciting Hutterite hymns and biblical passages. At age 14 children begin eating meals with the adults in the dining hall where they take the seat with the lowest position. After finishing the eighth grade or upon reaching age 16 children discontinue their schooling and begin working as adults.

Rollings hills near Malta. — Mark Thompson

THE MID HI-LINE

Beyond the Triangle, east of Havre, lies another distinctive slice of northern Montana, part of a vernacular region identifiable by most Eastern Montanans as the Hi-Line, or High-Line. This perceptual region roughly corresponds to the area bounded by the Missouri River on the south and the Canadian border to the north.

The name probably can be traced to the arrival of the Great Northern Railroad and the associated string of communities and tributary areas which developed in the 1880s and 1890s. Given a location high to the north within the state, and linear in shape, the name seems only logical. Today U.S. Highway 2 as well as the Burlington Northern Railroad are the two threads that tie this region together.

The western and eastern limits are less clear. To the west, the Hi-Line overlaps the northern part of our Triangle region. Geographer Ruth Hale, who mapped vernacular regions throughout the American Great Plains, identified a linear Hi-Line extending eastward from around Cut Bank. This suggests that residents in the north section of our Triangle area may first identify with the Hi-Line and only secondarily with the Golden Triangle. In the east, her Hi-Line terminated at an imaginary north-south line passing through Scobey and Poplar. Our Mid Hi-Line corresponds with the central portion of this region.

East of Havre, at the western edge of the Mid Hi-Line, the proportion of cropland drops off and the percentage of farmland devoted to range increases dramatically. Here, beyond the irrigated Milk River Valley, emphasis in most areas is on livestock rather than wheat and other grain crops. Grain fields become more scattered and ranch size ranges upward, not uncommonly totaling tens of thousands of acres. The resultant thinner population shows up on a state highway map. Away from U.S. Highway 2 towns are small and distantly spaced, and paved roads are the exception.

> More than two thirds of the Mid Hi-Line's population is in the string of communities along Highway 2 and within the adjacent lands hugging the Milk River.

More than two-thirds of the Mid Hi-Line's population is in the string of communities along Highway 2 and within the adjacent lands hugging the Milk River. This constitutes one of the state's major irrigated farming districts, where large sections were developed as part of the massive, federal Milk River Project in the early years of this century. In 1911 the first water flowed into what has now expanded to about 140,000 irrigated acres along the main stem of the Milk between Havre and Glasgow.

Initially the federal government had planned that twice that amount of land eventually would be irrigated, but closer inspection showed most soils unsuitable for irrigated farming. Although soils along the river range from very poor to very good, the bulk is poorer class soil with a high clay and salt content — undesirable qualities for intensive irrigated farming. Since the Missouri River once drained down this section of the Milk River Valley, perhaps it deserves the "blame." Still, these bottomlands are an integral part of the region's agricultural economy. Typically, a rancher who has bottomland acreage also has even more range and uses the bottomland as a feed base for the production of alfalfa hay and barley, and as a protected area to winter cattle.

Clockwise from Left: *If there's a Montana Community without a Stockman's Bar, it's an exception. Scenes from the Blaine County Fair.* — John Alwin photos

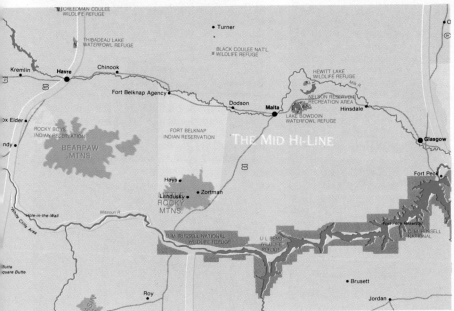

Clockwise from Above Left: *Fork Peck Lake provides water recreation on what some expect to be totally arid plains. Pelicans take to the wing at Bowdoin Wildlife Refuge. Robert Thorpe has been a train attendant for 33 years. (Of Eastern Montana he says, people have heard that it's dry and dusty and when they see a little green, they're really surprised.) U.S. Post Office at Dodson.* — John Alwin, Rick Graetz, John Alwin, John Alwin

Grain farmers in the Mid Hi-Line have the dubious distinction of having some of the most serious wind erosion problems in the state.

Grain farmers in the Mid Hi-Line have the dubious distinction for having some of the most serious wind erosion problems in the state. In 1980 Phillips County topped all other counties with 70,000 acres damaged by wind, and Blaine County checked in with a third-ranking 40,000 acres. That year, these two counties accounted for almost a third of the wind-damaged acres statewide. This has significant implications for loss of soil since wind erosion that is visibly detectable is eroding at the rate of at least 15 tons per acre per year. Reminiscent of the 1930s, locals report that during the dry summers of 1979 and 1980 clouds of blowing soil sometimes made it look as if the prairies were afire. State conservationist Van Haderlie with the U.S. Soil Conservation Service in Bozeman attributes a lot of the damage to excessive or improper cultivation.

The narrow, several-mile-wide band of towns and irrigated farmlands paralleling Highway 2 and the Milk River is a classic example of an Eastern Montana "sutland," separating "yonlands" to the north and south. Both terms were introduced in the 1950s by the late rural sociologist Carl Kraenzel while on the faculty at Montana State University. He saw these as the two major types of settings in which people live over much of the American Great Plains.

Sutlands are more densely settled areas, often linear in form, paralleling major rivers and lines of transportation and communication. There, irrigated agriculture usually dominates, towns are larger and more numerous, and transportation is best developed. Beyond the sutlands and literally "out yonder,"

is the yonland. Overall population density is much lower, towns are smaller and more widely spaced, transportation facilities are poorly developed, and agriculture is characteristically less intensive and based on livestock ranching and dryland farming.

Glasgow (pop. 4500), Malta (pop. 2400), and Chinook (pop. 1700) may be mere village-size communities in some parts of the nation, but in this section of northern Montana they are the largest urban centers. Each is seat for one of the three spacious counties which comprise this region. All have one of the three hospitals in the region and provide area residents with the most complete range of retail and professional services. They are the Mid Hi-Line's major shipping points for agricultural products.

As you head north or south out of this Milk River sutland, in most areas you leave pavement behind and begin to understand why the state highway map cautions travelers on some roads, "local inquiry may save time." Rural population density drops off dramatically, irrigated agriculture abruptly yields to range, and communities are small to non-existent. Turner (pop. 75-100), is the "metropolis" of the northern yonland. The only other communities here are Whitewater (pop. 50), Loring (pop. 25), and Hogeland (pop. 15). South of the Milk River sutland and between Highway 191 and the north shore of Fort Peck Reservoir is a 4,000-square-mile yonland without a single community or even a mile of paved highway! If you head into these areas, don't expect to find your favorite fast-food restaurant.

South of the Milk River and between Highway 191 and the north shore of Fort Peck Reservoir is a 4,000-square-mile yonland without a single community or even a mile of paved highway.

Still looking for a productive use, the abandoned Glasgow Air Force Base has entertained proposals for prisons, refugee resettlement, educational rehabilitation. —John Alwin

GLASGOW

Glasgow seems larger than its 1980 Census population of 4,500. A drive through nearby former Glasgow Air Force Base, which once housed more than 5,000 personnel, is an eerie reminder of the much larger regional population the town formerly served. Despite a decline over the last 20 years, Glasgow is still the largest community for a distance of almost 120 miles in all directions. The local chamber of commerce places all of Montana's northeastern corner, and even sections of southern Saskatchewan, within the town's trade area.

Named after Glasgow, Scotland, it was another railroad siding along the Hi-Line which evolved into a town, beginning as a tent town in 1887. Designation as division point on the Great Northern, coupled with its strategic location astride the "boundaries" between livestock ranching to the west and south, cash grain farming to the north and east, and irrigated agriculture in the adjacent Milk River Valley helped assure its ascendence. During the first two decades of this century the population increased by almost 500 percent, climbing to more than 2,000 by 1920. It swelled even more during the 1930s when thousands swarmed into the area to work on the colossal Fort Peck project.

Population peaked prior to the 1968-69 closing of sprawling Glasgow Air Force Base. The impact of this closure is vividly reflected in the town's census figures which show a decline from 6,398 in 1960 to 4,700 in 1970. The base was officially deactivated in 1976, and three years later title for the 6,800-acre facility passed to Valley County to be operated as the Valley Industrial Park.

Finding major tenants has proved to be a real challenge to those in charge. Until its recent departure, the Family Training Center, a government-funded program to help disadvantaged families of a six-state area, had been the major occupant. Even at its maximum, the 100 families involved occupied only a tiny portion of the base's 1,250 living units. Present uses include a drug treatment center in the former base hospital, and aircraft and molasses storage. Following the eruption of Mount St. Helens, Boeing expanded its training flight operations at the base to escape the volcanic ash which would have damaged jet engines at their eastern Washington training center. At the time of this writing, the on-again, off-again plan to relocate 400-600 Cuban refugees at the base is apparently off.

Mike Goff, administrative assistant for the Valley Industrial Park, feels the facility is best suited for some type of aircraft industry, perhaps related to assembly or large-scale testing programs, but almost any type of manufacturing is being pursued. It seems the former base has the potential to be either an ace-in-the-hole or a white elephant for Glasgow and the citizenry of Valley County.

TURNER

When Turner-area residents need a length of rope or nuts and bolts, the procedure is simple. You go to McCracken's Grocery Shop downtown and borrow the key to Turner Hardware, across the street. You let yourself in, find what you need, lock up the store, return to McCracken's and pay for the items. Since the hardware store also has the town's only gas pumps, you follow the same procedure, the main power switch being inside the store. After filling your tank you turn off the master switch inside the hardware, lock up the store and report your sale to the clerk at McCracken's.

Turner is the epitome of a yonland community. Located 32 miles north of Harlem and 12 miles south of the Canadian line, it is the most convenient town for people on the 70 to 80 farms and ranches in the surrounding 500-square-mile area. In addition to the grocery and hardware stores, the center also boasts a grade school and high school, lumberyard, a Lutheran Church (a reflection of the dominance of Scandinavian ancestry), a more recent Christian Church, and Glen's Border Bar. Webster's ought to print a separate listing for the word "bar" to define places like Glen's. More than just a drinking establishment, Glen's is the town's meeting place for people of all ages. Lifetime area resident Nellie Obrecht certifies that "it's the social center in Turner." It is the only place in town to buy a cup of coffee and it sells the only pizza and hamburgers in the Mid Hi-Line's 5,000-square-mile yonland north of the Milk River Valley and Highway 2. On Sundays, when sale of liquor is prohibited in Saskatchewan, Canadians from towns like Frontier, Climax and Bracken help assure the bar one of its best days of the week.

The territory surrounding Turner is one of the few cash grain farming areas in the entire Mid Hi-Line. Its fertile soils produce wheat noted for its consistently high protein content. But both of the town's grain elevators are closed now and a train hasn't made it up the spur line as far as Turner in years. The railroad has officially initiated efforts to abandon the line. Grain producers have no choice now but to truck their crops to Harlem or Havre. The closest sale yard for cattle is 52 miles away in Chinook, but rancher Pete Watkins does buy and sell cattle locally.

MALTA

Pulling into Malta off U.S. Highway 2, the first evidence that you're entering yet another town whose history is closely linked to the railroad is the dip in the road as it drops under the railroad overpass. Like other communities along the Mid Hi-Line, Malta evolved from a railroad siding along the Great Northern. One would think these siding towns would be carbon copies of one another, but each has developed its own character and personality.

For Malta that identity has been closely linked to cattle. During the era of the open range it was hub for the northern Montana cattle industry where countless trail-worn cowboys, and later sheepmen, looking for a good time found it in the town's saloons and red-light section. Dryland and irrigation farmers displaced some cattlemen in the early 1900s, but even today Phillips County annual cash receipts from sale of livestock are almost twice that of crops.

The community's traditionally agricultural-based economy received a new component in 1979 when American Colloid began operation of its bentonite plant just east of town. Overnight it became the area's major private employer. Bentonite is a useful clay mineral that is an altered form of volcanic ash. In Eastern Montana it is mined from Cretaceous age rocks, the bentonite layers corresponding to accumulations of volcanic ash which probably settled to the bottom near the shore of an inland sea more than 60,000,000 years ago. There are several bentonite mines scattered around Eastern Montana. American Colloid mines its clay from an area about 25 miles south of Malta. The bentonite is trucked to town where it is dried, milled, blended, and mixed with chemicals prior to bagging. Shipped throughout the nation and overseas, the product has literally a thousand uses — rotary drilling muds for oil and gas exploration, binder for concentrating low grade iron ore (taconite pellets), and other uses ranging from cosmetics, to explosives, to filters for clarifying wines.

Above left: *Phillips County Courthouse.* — John Alwin

Above: *Malta grain elevators in early morning light.* — John Alwin

ZORTMAN

Who says the last of the mining boom towns in Montana's mountain gulches faded in the late 1800s? Nestled in a steep-sided and heavily forested narrow valley on the east side of the Little Rockies is Zortman, a modern gold and silver camp.

As the Little Rockies formed, intrusives cracked overlying sedimentary rocks. In the process, low-temperature waters carrying minerals in solution were forced up into these fissures. Minerals precipitated out and accumulated on fissure walls, sometimes completely filling the voids. It is these deposits that contain the gold and silver that attracted miners to the area.

Mining already had lured job seekers to Zortman by 1903 when a cyanide mill was built for leaching gold from two area mines, one soon connected to its plant by aerial tramway. Following the construction of the mill, things really started happening. New workers moved in to fill jobs at the plant and in support areas, working for wages of between $3.00 and $4.00 per day. A stage line began regular service between Malta and Zortman and the community was blessed with a post office. The number and variety of local business establishments expanded and by 1907 the town had its own newspaper, the *Little Rockies Miner*. Writing in his first edition, the editor proclaimed Zortman the "metropolis of the Little Rockies," estimating that the town had 200 houses and a population of 400. Heavily guarded wagons loaded with gold bars could soon be seen lumbering along the road enroute to the Great Northern shipping points of Malta and Dodson. In the summer of 1907, the *Little Rockies Miner* optimistically speculated that Zortman's population might grow to 5,000. It may have peaked at around 800 during the next decade, but then went downhill. Gold shipments stopped altogether in 1949.

By the 1970s Zortman had a year-round population of about ten families. A general store and a combination bar/cafe were the only retail establishments, and their success depended heavily on non-locals — summer trade of the curious who came to see a real western mining ghost town, overnighters at the nearby state campground, hunters, and Christmas tree seekers from Malta, Glasgow and other Hi-Line communities.

Zortman has usually made it into the standard ghost town books. Its rickety old, weather-worn buildings provided tourists with a photo opportunity in an honest-to-goodness ghost town. Then, in 1979-80, rapidly rising gold prices brought renewed life.

In 1979 Landusky Mining began operating in the area and the next year Zortman Mining Company followed. The companies operated three truck-and-shovel, open pit mines in 1981 and produced 38,000 ounces of gold and more than 100,000 ounces of silver. Local population in Zortman balloons to 300 during the summer production peak. Mining activity now employs approximately 160 people, more than can be housed in Zortman. Many live in trailers and pick-up campers, modern day counterparts to the more rustic log cabins of yesterday's miners. The surrounding federally owned Bureau of Land Management property has made it difficult for the town to acquire much needed building space. Some miners live as far away as Malta and commute to and from Zortman.

The mining companies are happy to conduct tours from May to September. Mine manager Ed Roper suggests people call in advance to find out specifics on days and times of tours.

Above: *Zortman from the air showing the impact on the community of mining activity.* — Ken Turner

Right: *Zortman has preserved the flavor of its early history — here the Zortman jail.* — Rick Graetz

Below: *The road to Zortman.* — Rick Graetz

FORT BELKNAP RESERVATION

The Indian nations of the Gros Ventre and Assiniboine are now at home on the Fort Belknap Reservation. From 1855 to 1888 they shared the extensive hunting lands north of the Missouri with their Blackfeet neighbors to the west. This was to remain their territory for a period of 99 years, but pressure from white settlers clamoring for more land led to a cession agreement with the United States after only 33 years. In 1888 the two tribes accepted a much smaller reservation in exchange for slightly more than $1,000,000 which they were to receive from the government over a ten-year period.

The irregular southern border of today's reservation looks as if someone took a bite out of it in the area of the Little Rockies, which is precisely what happened. Discovery of mineral deposits in what became the Zortman-Landusky area prompted an 1896 agreement to cede the gold-rich area back to the federal government. That final land cession reduced the reservation to its present size of about 617,000 acres.

Enrollment of both tribes now totals approximately 3,900, about half of whom live on and immediately adjacent to the reservation. The majority of reservation Indians live in the southern section of the reserve in and around the communities of Hays, Lodgepole, and Big Beaver. The 1980 Census also counted almost 300 Indians in Harlem, just north of the reservation where they account for about one-third of the town's population.

Fully three-fourths of the reservation is used for grazing, about one-fifth for cropland (mostly spring wheat), and the remainder is commercial forest land. There is now talk of a possible bentonite mine and preliminary discussions relating to oil and gas exploration are underway, but agriculture probably will hold the key to future economic development, since the reservation evidently lacks the extensive proven mineral resources of some other Montana Indian lands.

ROCKY BOYS INDIAN RESERVATION

Montana's Rocky Boys Reservation is the state's newest and smallest. Created in 1916 by Congressional action it is home to what is today called the Chippewa Cree Tribe, an amalgam of Chippewa and Cree bands who migrated westward from the Great Lakes area. In the late 1800s and early 1900s they wandered about Montana and adjacent sections of Canada without a home base, living largely a hand-to-mouth existence, commonly visiting area towns in search of hand outs. Many Montanans considered them "Canadian Indians" but when Congress appropriated funds to have them deported to Canada, most returned. Concern for their welfare led to the creation of the initial 55,000-acre reservation on a portion of the old Fort Assiniboine Military Reserve.

Since then the reservation has been expanded to just over 107,000 acres and tribal membership has grown to some 2,700 with about half usually residing on the reservation, many living in and around Rocky Boys Agency.

Like other Montana reservations, the Rocky Boys has a serious unemployment problem. Bureau of Indian Affairs Administration Officer Joe Monteau estimated unemployment at 75 percent in early 1982. Tribal members can obtain free-use assignments to 160-acre parcels, and half the reservation is so designated, but it is difficult to get by on such a small acreage. To help develop the reservation's economic base, the tribe has started Dry Forks Farms, a cooperative to which many locals lease their land.

The tribe has also developed a ski area in the forested Bear Paw Mountains in the southern part of the reservation. Eastern Montana's only downhill facility, its three runs provide regional ski enthusiasts with the state's most economical downhill skiing.

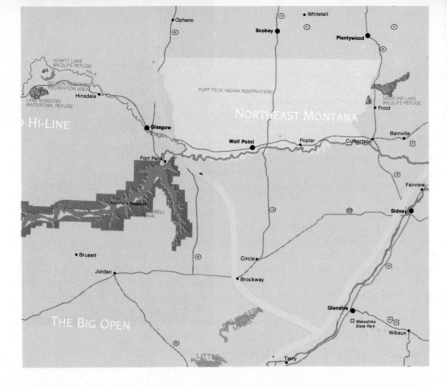

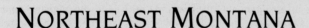

NORTHEAST MONTANA

Northeast Montana stands out as the only extensive grain farming region in the state's eastern half. In this area the continental ice sheet pushed south just beyond the Missouri River, softening the landscape as far south as the northern sections of McCone and Richland counties. This subdued topography, coupled with a mantle of fertile soils, help make this glaciated area excellent land for small grain farming. Even within the section of Northeast Montana beyond the southern margin of the former ice sheet, grain farming is widespread. Most years three of Northeast Montana's counties rank in the top half-dozen of the state's leading wheat-producing counties. To the west in the Mid Hi-Line and Big Open, less favorable soil qualities, lower precipitation and often rougher topography rule out heavy emphasis on cash grain farming except in favored locales.

The Northeast is part of a large international Spring Wheat Belt that begins in South Dakota and extends to the northwest through North Dakota and into the Canadian prairie provinces of Manitoba, Saskatchewan, and Alberta. Montana's northeastern corner falls just within the belt's western fringe. Rather than an emphasis on winter wheat, as in the Golden Triangle, emphasis here is on spring wheat owing to the characteristically harsh winters that would be damaging to

winter wheat. Only in the southern section does winter wheat become a prevalent crop.

> The Northeast is part of a large international Spring Wheat Belt that begins in South Dakota and extends to the northwest into the Canadian prairie provinces.

The better suited agricultural land is able to support a more dense population. This is reflected on the state highway map which shows the area with a much higher density of roads than in the Mid Hi-Line or the Big Open. The close spacing of grain-elevator punctuated communities along rail lines, such as Opheim, Glentana, Richland, Peerless, Four Buttes, and Scobey along the last 46 miles of a Burlington Northern branch line, is similar to the Golden Triangle. Like its grain-growing counterpart to the west, the Northeast is facing saline seep, rail abandonment and unit trains, and declining small, rural service centers.

This region is located on the western flank of the Williston Basin, and commercial energy production has been a part of the economic picture since the 1950s when oil discoveries were made in several counties. As in other sections of Montana's far eastern border area, this region is experiencing another energy boom, as oil companies search beneath the prairie for oil that was missed or passed over in the 1950s.

Future energy development has the potential to literally remake the geography of the area. Rather than oil, this future might well be based on exploitation of the huge quantities of strippable lignite that underlie much of the region. There are plans for a synthetic fuels plant at Circle. The plant would cover approximately 100 acres of land and process locally mined lignite into liquid fuel. The Burlington Northern's Circle West proposal, as it has been called, has run into opposition from some locals who are concerned about environmental qualities and the overall impact on the largely rural and thinly populated area. The scale of such an operation is mind boggling. A 30,000-barrel-per-day plant and associated mining and service employment probably would result in the addition of as many as 10,000 permanent new residents. That would mean more than a 1000 percent increase in Circle's population!

Great Blue Heron young taken at Medicine Lake Wildlife Refuge. — Calvin Larsen

MEDICINE LAKE NATIONAL WILDLIFE REFUGE

Medicine Lake is one of several Eastern Montana wildlife refuges administered by the U.S. Fish and Wildlife Service. It is not the largest or smallest, but is typical of many.

Created in 1935, the refuge covers about 50 square miles in two parcels, with approximately 40 percent of it covered by water. Prior to development, Medicine Lake was really only a shallow marsh which receded each fall exposing alkaline mud flats. Funds appropriated by Congress and work by the WPA and CCC camps resulted in water-control structures that hold back spring rains, making possible a more controlled 8,700-acre lake. It, 1,280-acre Homestead Lake in the southern tract, and other smaller lakes and potholes, provide valuable habitat for migrating geese and ducks.

A location in the Central Flyway assures heavy usage by migrating birds. The refuge also serves as an important breeding ground for waterfowl and other birds. The feed supply on the refuge is supplemented by the several hundred acres that are farmed through a cooperative agreement with local farmers. Sharecroppers grow mostly wheat, barley, and some field corn in strip-cropped fields within the refuge. The refuge's share of the crops is left in the fields to provide food for wildlife and to help minimize depradation on neighboring farmers' fields.

Birdlife is abundant and varied, especially during the spring and fall migration periods. Some of the most common nesting birds include Canada geese, mallards, gadwalls, pintails, blue-winged teal and canvasback. In early summer birdwatchers are treated to large colonies of white pelicans, great blue herons and double-crested cormorants. A check list of more than 200 species observed on the refuge is available at the headquarters on the northwest shore of Medicine Lake. This is a good place to start the self-guided auto tour through the most scenic portion of the refuge. For those not afflicted with acrophobia, a climb to the top of the 100-foot observation tower provides a panoramic vista and excellent visual orientation to the refuge.

PLENTYWOOD

Plentywood, Montana is an international playground, of sorts. You won't find British, Japanese, or West German tourists who jet in to view the surrounding golden wheat fields, or jet setters dropping in from Monte Carlo, but there are plenty of Canadians who drive the 125 miles south from Regina, Saskatchewan, or other nearby areas, looking for a break and good time.

On some summer weekends, Canadians account for up to a third of the guests in some of the town's motels. Their numbers have been down lately, undoubtedly, in part, because of the very unfavorable exchange rate (20 percent in early 1982).

Entertainment has been the major draw. Joan Melcher points out in her popular and practical, *Watering Hole: A User's Guide to Montana Bars*, that "Plentywood has developed its own breed of saloon — ultra modern, all-purpose and huge . . . It seems the idea is to hold on to customers by providing all the vital services in one building — food, drink, dancing and entertainment — to say nothing of gambling, which is something folks in Plentywood try to say nothing about." Here Canadians can do things that are illegal back home in Saskatchewan. They, as well as locals, can drink on Sundays, drink and dance in the same room, and get in a little gambling.

About three years ago the FBI raided two Plentywood saloons and confiscated more than $18,000 in currency and $10,000 in gambling chips. Canadian stuke poker, a variant of Blackjack, had been popular until the raids, but is now illegal. Gambling is still a part of the local entertainment scene, but is supposed to be limited to poker and poker machines.

Plentywood is attractive and clean, and reminds some visitors of Canadian towns. Consistent with that characteristic, it probably has more garden flowers per person than any other Montana town. The community's penchant for flowers is reflected in the fact that Plentywood has two flower shops, even though its population is just 2,500.

In the 1950s Plentywood participated in the energy boom that gripped extreme Eastern Montana. Skyrocketing energy prices and a push toward greater energy self-sufficiency in the United States during the 1970s induced oil companies to return to the Williston Basin to renew their search. Oil production in the county has risen from 116,000 barrels in 1957 to 3.5 million barrels in 1980. According to a recent *Plentywood Herald* story, oil now accounts for 82 percent of Sheridan County's taxable valuation. A new 120-unit, mobile home park is projected to go in on the south side of town in the summer of 1982 to help ease the housing crunch linked to the oil boom.

Plentywood emanates an air of prosperity despite its somewhat off-the-main-track and corner location within Montana. Historically its county seat status and the productive spring wheat lands in Sheridan County allowed it to prosper. The economics of wheat farming have been erratic at best in recent years, but unlike some other towns, Plentywood has been able to thrive, at least in part because of a more varied economic base.

Top: *Downtown Plentywood — perhaps more garden and floral stores per person than anywhere else in Montana.* — John Alwin

Bottom: *Port of Raymond.* — John Alwin

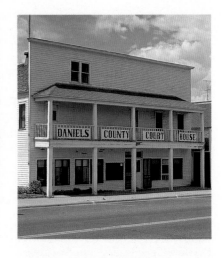

Clockwise from Upper Left: *Highway 16 north of Plentywood. Scobey boasts the state's only curling facility. The Daniels County Courthouse. East of Bainville. Threshing Bee — John Alwin, Milton Gunderson, John Alwin, Jim Romo, Montana Travel Promotion Unit*

FORT PECK RESERVATION

The Fort Peck Reservation was created in 1887 at the same time as the Blackfeet and Fort Belknap reservations farther west. That year the 20,000,000-acre joint reservation for the Blackfeet, Assiniboine, Sioux and Gros Ventre tribes was surrendered and these three much smaller parcels were allocated to the tribes. In 1888 the present Fort Peck Reservation boundaries were established, and it became home for members of both the Assiniboine and Sioux tribes.

Even though the reservation set aside 2,000,000 acres for the Fort Peck tribes, less than half remains in their control. Loss of the land dates back to earlier this century when white homesteaders spilled into this fertile northeastern corner of Montana. Pressure was put on Congress to open up the reservation to homesteaders, and in 1907 the United States government signed an agreement with the Fort Peck tribes for the allotment of the reservation and sale of surplus lands. Each Indian was entitled to 320 acres of grazing land plus some timber and irrigable lands. But most of the land left after allotments were made was disposed of under the United States homestead laws, which in effect opened the reservation to white settlers.

The Assiniboine and Sioux have been trying to regain their reservation and have purchased tens of thousands of acres. In the mid-1970s the tribes got back 86,000 acres of "submarginal" lands that had been abandoned by homesteaders in the 1920s and 1930s and were then held by the federal government until 1975.

The inroads of non-Indians on the reservation can be seen in the largest town of Wolf Point. The 1980 Census showed 3,074 residents, but only 709 were Indian. Even in Poplar, headquarters for the tribes, Indians make up less than half the population. All totaled, there are now about 7,500 enrolled members of both tribes, over half of whom live on the reservation. An additional 500 Indians, mostly Cree and Chippewa from North Dakota, add to Indian numbers.

The reservation's economy is based primarily on beef cattle and wheat. But since much of the better reservation crop land now belongs to whites, Indian agriculture traditionally has emphasized livestock.

Each summer six Indian celebrations are held on the Fort Peck Reservation. Locally, the biggest is the Oil Discovery Celebration, which is held at the campground north of Poplar. The festival began in 1952 after the discovery of oil on the reservation. Nationally, it is the Wolf Point Wild Horse Stampede that draws more attention. Begun as an all-Indian rodeo more than 50 years ago it is now considered a major event that consistently attracts National Finals caliber contestants.

Far Left: *Sioux Indian Dancer.* — Courtesy of Montana Promotion Unit

Left: *A smoke shop near Poplar. Indians on several Montana reservations sell tobacco, which is not subject to state excise tax on the reservations, at a reduced price. It is illegal for non-tribal members to possess cigarettes without a state tax stamp.* — John Alwin

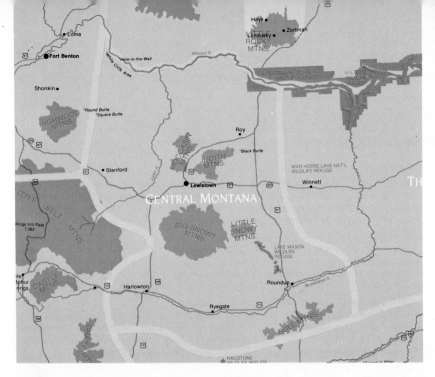

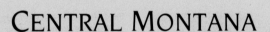

CENTRAL MONTANA

Ask the people in Lewistown whether they think they live in Eastern or Western Montana and you would probably get a reply something like, "neither, we live in Central Montana." Residents of the community and its surrounding area sense an identity with that region, which may be as much a reflection of location within the state as it is a perception of a distinctive vernacular region. When given the choice of an either/or response, most select Eastern Montana, although the proximity of mountains makes an eastern answer less than unanimous. This is one Eastern Montana region that clearly overlaps into Western Montana and probably could be extended to include the Little Belt Mountains and Smith River Valley area.

Central Montana is rich in history that includes virtually all phases of Montana's colorful past. Today it has representatives of many types of economic activity that are found throughout the entire state. More than any other section of the state, this region is a microcosm of Montana.

More than any other region, it is a microcosm of Montana.

94

Opposite Page Top: *Between Rapelje and Ryegate.* — Rick Graetz

Bottom: *East of Lewistown.* — Mark Thompson

Right: *Lewistown area.* — Rick Graetz

For thousands of years the lush grasses of the Judith Basin and forested mountains were preferred hunting areas for Indians and later fur trappers and traders who sought the plentiful supply of small game. By the 1870s the white men had started moving cattle onto the luxuriant prairie, probing and testing the suitability of these lands for livestock. To few people's surprise, cattle thrived, and soon large ranches and thousands of head populated the basin. Before long, the white population of stockmen and settlers was sufficient to merit protection from potentially hostile natives, and soldiers were stationed at Camp Lewis and later at Fort Maginnis.

The first major influx of population into the area had to await the discovery of gold in the highly mineralized Judith Mountains. The original discovery was made on the west side of the range in 1880, and a predictably large army of prospectors converged on the diggings. Within a year the new camp of Maiden may have had a population of 6,000! The easily obtained deposits were quickly exhausted, and operations then shifted to quartz, or hard rock mining. This meant underground mining, mills, and a much greater permanence than is normally associated with placer mining communities.

In 1885 Maiden vied with Lewistown for designation as seat of Fergus County. Its case was a valid one since the community's population of several hundred made it the largest in the newly created county. Support from stockmen and ranchers in the basin tipped the scale in favor of Lewistown, but it is interesting to speculate what might have happened had the mining town won out. Without county seat status, the community dwindled, and when a fire destroyed most of the town in 1905, there was no point in rebuilding since most residents already had moved on.

Other mining towns appeared in the mountains outside Lewistown. Giltedge, on the east side of the Judiths, assumed prominence there in the early 1890s following construction of a large mill to process local ores. By 1900-01 it had a population of 350 and sported citified, wooden sidewalks. Mining and population peaked in 1908-09 and then subsided.

Kendall was a somewhat later mining town which took form across the valley at the foot of the North Moccasin Mountains. By 1901 the new camp was taking shape and, soon, substantial stone buildings graced the town's thoroughfare, some with electricity. In 1902 daily stage service linked the community with Lewistown. One estimate places the town's population at 1,000 in 1910, and by 1913 production from area mines helped make Fergus County the number one gold producer in the state. Production dropped dramatically in the later Teens, and like other area mining towns, Kendall was on its way to its ghost town status. The town now belongs to the Boy Scouts of America and is being developed as a camp in a style consistent with the integrity of the site. Who knows, perhaps the renewal of mining and exploration just above old Kendall might result in Kendall II.

While these surrounding mines were in operation, Lewistown benefited from additional commerce. Well before their demise, however, the agricultural sector of the basin already had become much more important to the regional economy and to that of the town. The arrival of rail service in the early 1900s practically guaranteed the prosperity of both.

Central Montana is still primarily an agricultural region. The industry ranges from irrigated farming along the Musselshell and Judith rivers, to large-scale, cash grain farming in the northwest, to even more extensive areas of livestock ranching. Cattle and sheep are still the number one dollar generators in Fergus and Musselshell counties and livestock generally produces more than twice the cash receipts of crops.

Above Left: *Hutterite woman, downtown Lewistown.* **Above Right:** *Tom Morrison unloading a wheat truck, Garneill.* —John Alwin

Below: *West of Stanford.* —Mark Thompson

Opposite Page: *West of Grass Range.* —Jim Romo

In 1881 a new trading post was built at the site of the Story Fort. First called Reed's Fort, after the postmaster and then post owner, it provided the local populace with supplies and mail service. Other buildings were soon added, including a hotel and blacksmith shop and, of course, saloons. For awhile the young community was known as "Lewiston," but the spelling was changed to "Lewistown" in 1884.

Lewistown grew with the influx of ranchers and farmers in the last two decades of the 1800s, but development was held back because of the lack of local rail service, a problem rectified in 1903 with the belated arrival of the Central Montana Railroad. The railroad linked the area with outside markets and proved to be the key that unlocked its rich and varied resources. Other lines followed, and by 1920 Lewistown had more than 6,100 residents and ranked as Eastern Montana's fourth largest town.

Lewistown continues unchallenged as nexus of Central Montana. This town of 7,000 and its setting are among the most attractive in Eastern Montana. Surrounded by forested mountains on three sides, the Moccasins, the Judiths, and the Big Snowys, the setting is a unique one for Eastern Montana.

Locals claim title to exact geographical center of the state and pinpoint the precise spot at the site of the Christian Church parsonage on Main Street. Perhaps it is this centrality, coupled with the small-city character and vacationland surroundings that make this an increasingly popular retirement spot.

Lewistown does not, however, fit the stereotype of a retirement community. Says Bonnie Cornett, editor of the *Lewistown News Argus*, "It's an active little town." It is home to the annual Central Montana Fair, Rodeo and Horse Show, held the last week of July. In late March for over 35 years the town has also been the site for the now highly regarded Western Invitational Tournament. College basketball's *crème de la crème* of seniors and recent graduates from throughout the West and Midwest form teams hoping to pique the interest of an attending NBA scout or, at least, enjoying an extended playing season. Joining the professional scouts is a predictably boisterous crowd which jams into the Lewistown Civic Center's small gymnasium at tourney time. The four-day affair provides the sponsoring local Jaycees with thousands of dollars in profit, most of which is pumped back into the community.

Each Labor Day weekend the colorful Metis Celebration reminds locals of the town's unusual heritage. Lewistown's many stately sandstone buildings are an ever-present reminder of the contribution of yet another group of immigrants — of Croatian stone masons who arrived between 1898 and 1915.

Another link with the region's past is the commercial mining just south of town. Instead of the glitter of gold and silver of bygone days, U.S. Gypsum's mine produces the more mundane, but highly useful gypsum, which it manufactures into gypsum wall board (sheet rock) at the site. The underground mine and plant facility provides jobs for about 100 people and is the area's second largest private employer, after the new Central Montana Hospital.

LEWISTOWN

It was a strategic location, good farmland, and a picturesque setting that explained Lewistown's origin a century ago and the same features are mainly responsible for its continuing dominance within Central Montana.

The first structure in the immediate vicinity was a trading post known as the Story Fort. Built by Bozemanites Nelson Story and Charles Hoffman in 1873, it operated for only a year.

The founders of what was to become Lewistown arrived from Canada in 1879. They were a group of about forty families of Metis, French Canadian-Indian mixed bloods. These immigrants had fled from the western Canadian province of Manitoba where some had most likely participated in a short-lived rebellion under Louis Riel. This was to be their promised land, situated near the Carroll Road, a vital link between Helena and a steamship port on the Missouri above the mouth of the Musselshell, and located within the fertile and scenic Judith Basin.

ROUNDUP

Yugoslavian surnames like Ratvovic, Bublich, and Antonich, and Polish names such as Marsinkowski, Cowalski, and Cowalczyk are commonplace in Roundup and have been since early this century. Descendents of the Eastern Europeans who immigrated by the hundreds to work in area coal mines, they are now part of the ethnic mosaic that imparts a distinctive character to this southeastern corner of Central Montana.

A nearby place called "Roundup" actually predates the existing town of the same name. It was essentially a stage depot and post office just west of today's townsite. The post office began operation in 1883, during the open range era, and served big ranches in the fertile grazing lands along the Musselshell and northward to the Snowy Mountains. The name evidently derives from the fact that this was a place where cattle roundups centered, the natural basin and its abundant forage providing a good place to drive cattle for holding.

The present town of Roundup didn't really get started until 1907-08 when the Chicago, Milwaukee, and St. Paul Railroad built its Pacific Coast extension up the Musselshell. The sub-bituminous coal of the Bull Mountains had been known of for decades, and its presence was clearly a factor in the extension of the railroad's line through the area. The Milwaukee needed Roundup coal to fuel its steam locomotives since the Bull Mountains field was the only major source along its right-of-way between Iowa and the Cle Elum area on the east slope of Washington's Cascade Mountains.

The railroad, through its Republic Coal Company subsidiary, opened its first mine in 1907, but abandoned that site in 1908 in favor of one just a couple of miles south and west of the embryonic town of Roundup. This was designated the Number 2 mine, around which the town of Klein quickly developed. The Number 3 mine was started in 1908 by the Roundup Mining Company closer to town, near where U.S. Highway 87 crosses the Musselshell. Another "town" soon took form adjacent to this mine, called Camp 3. Other mines and associated small communities developed in the area, but 2 and 3 were the major operations, and together may have employed as many as 2,000 miners.

Since 1911 the Roundup field has been the state's second ranking producer. Production reached near record levels during World War II, but then declined in the 1950s and 1960s with the closure of all major mines. Phasing in of diesel locomotives and a general switch by residential and commercial consumers to other energy sources, like oil and gas, eliminated previous markets.

Today only two small, open-pit mines operate near the divide in the Bull Mountains. Because of this readily available and relatively inexpensive fuel, many homes in Roundup are still heated with coal. These mines also supply fuel to an increasing number of energy-conscious domestic and commercial users from Billings to Bozeman.

Although the major mines are now history, they and their workers have had a permanent impact on the Roundup area. At Klein, two large cemeteries on either side of Highway 89 are somber reminders of the hazards of earlier underground mining. During the holiday season, *Potiza*, a native Yugoslavian sweet bread made with a walnut filling, is a local favorite. Long before home wine making came into vogue, many residents of Yugoslavian descent were brewing their extra strong *Grappo*. Traditional wedding ceremonies that can last for days still observe the custom of pinning money to the dress of the dancing bride.

Top: *Early Croation immigrants in the Roundup area built stone houses in the* nearby cliffs. **Bottom:** *The Roy football field.* — John Alwin

Roundup has been able to maintain a remarkably stable population over the last half century. The 1980 Census showed it to be a town of 2,119, just three more than in 1970. It is now the unrivaled trade center for the surrounding area in which emphasis is clearly on livestock.

As in many other Eastern Montana communities, the late 1970s and early 1980s witnessed an energy boom. Motels are commonly filled to overflowing with oil people, and an oil-service company is now the largest local employer. Recent plans that would have revived large-scale underground coal mining in the Bull Mountains have been abandoned, but locals are still hoping such mining might materialize when and if demand for coal improves. The project also would mean rail service for the community, which has been without a railroad since the Milwaukee discontinued its Montana network in 1980.

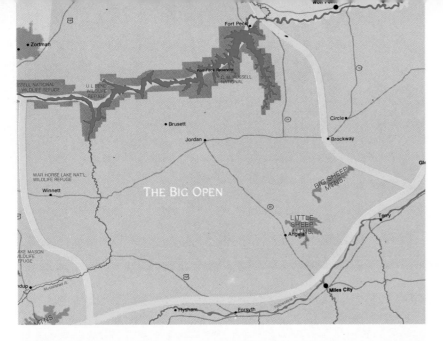

Long distances to services still is a fact of life in the Big Open.
Courtesy Foster-Jordan Drug

Opposite: *Piney Buttes near Jordan.* — Rick Graetz

THE BIG OPEN

The "Big Open" is a term borrowed from the noted, late 19th-century photographer, L. A. Huffman of Miles City. This was his name for the expansive wedge-shaped portion of Montana prairie between the Yellowstone and Missouri rivers. Other city residents simply called that region the "North Side," as opposed to the "South Side" of the Yellowstone — a reflection of Miles City's prominence in Eastern Montana at that time.

Driving west beyond Circle and Brockway on State Highway 200 it is apparent that land use changes. Grain fields are more infrequent and rangeland comes to dominate. There is an obvious decrease in population density. A highway traveler does not pass through, or even near, a town along the 55-mile stretch between Brockway and Jordan. Except for Winnett (pop. 207), 76 miles further west along Highway 200, and Melstone (pop. approximately 150) further to the south on U.S. Highway 12, there are no other towns. Highway maps do show places like Brusett, Angela, Mosby, and Sumatra, but most are little more than rural post offices, sometimes in association with a general store/gas station.

This expansive yonland area, corresponding with Garfield County and adjacent portions of McCone, Prairie, Custer, Rosebud and Petroleum counties, was dubbed "Jordan Country" a half century ago by then-president of the American Geographical Society Isaiah Bowman. He had been lured west to the area in 1930 in conjunction with research for a book he was writing on pioneering life. Bowman found just what he was looking for. The region had a widely dispersed population of less than one person per square mile, still living a characteristically pioneering life of experimentation and unsettlement. One medical doctor served the entire region, and Jordan Country was without rail or bus service, had no phone or telegraph, and lacked all-weather roads. His classic 1931 article based on his findings gave international recognition to the region and geographers worldwide know about the Jordan Country of 1930.

Isaiah Bowman's Jordan Country obviously has changed over the last 50 years. But even though the pioneering life which characterized that area is gone, Bowman taking a golden anniversary look at the same region would have found largely unchanged a surprising number of the regional characteristics that had attracted him a half century earlier, especially those relating to transportation, medical care, and schooling.

During Bowman's 1930 visit Jordanites and those in the surrounding area were eagerly awaiting the arrival of rail service. The previous fall the presidents of both the Great Northern and Northern Pacific had been in town extolling the attributes of their projected lines. Neither railroad built through Jordan Country, nor did any others, and to this day, the area remains railless. In fact, the region is even worse off now than it was in 1930 since the 1980 abandonment of the Chicago, Milwaukee, St. Paul and Pacific track which passed through Ingomar and Sumatra in this southern sector of Jordan Country. Just as in 1930, the branch line of another carrier terminates at Brockway, 55 miles to the east, and is still as close as the railroad comes to Jordan. To the north the nearest railroad service is beyond Fort Peck Reservoir, and the Lewistown area is as close as a rail approaches from the west.

> A highway traveler does not pass through, or even near, a town along the 55-mile stretch between Brockway and Jordan.

Winnett, next town to the east, Jordan 76 miles. — Mark Thompson

Transportation remains a serious problem for most residents. Ranchers and farmers have no choice but to truck their products to adjacent sutland towns such as Miles City or Billings. Since local population is insufficient to justify regular airline or even bus service, locals without their own cars are severely hampered. With federal assistance, Jordan has been able to develop its own transportation system. Twice each month residents can ride their 12-passenger mini-bus the 85 miles to Miles City. Although intended primarily to provide free transportation for senior citizens, others are welcome to go along on the all-day outing for a $5 fare, provided there is room. Once a month, or at least every other month, the same bus makes the 350-mile round trip to Billings. Passengers leave at 6 a.m. and return around 10 p.m. the same night. The fare for non-seniors is $10.

If Jordanites are without their own transportation and need more frequent Miles City connections, there are only two regularly available options. They can ride the mail truck which carries mail between Jordan and Miles City six days a week. The driver gets into Jordan around 8 a.m. every day but Sunday and departs at 4:30 p.m. The one-way trip costs about $5. On Sunday the only available transportation is with the delivery man who brings in the Billings newspaper and returns to Miles around noon.

> Dr. B. C. Farrand of Jordan arrived in the '20s and remained the only practicing doctor in a 7,000-square-mile area until his retirement in the '70s.

At the time of Bowman's visit, Dr. B. C. Farrand of Jordan was the only practicing medical doctor in the 7,000-square-mile area. Dr. Farrand had arrived in the middle '20s and remained the region's only doctor through the early 1970s. He recalls Bowman's visit and can now look back over 50 years of change in the county's health services. He was instrumental in the acquisition of the community's first hospital in 1928, and recalls it was initially difficult to convince residents to use the new facility. At the time he was thankful for the relative youth and generally good health of residents, most of whom had arrived as homesteaders within the previous 15 years. In 1943 he and the town druggist purchased a small plane which the doctor used until the late 1950s to reach more remote patients. Dr. Farrand also helped establish the community's present 28-bed hospital. In emergency cases when local facilities are inadequate, the county ambulance can have patients in Miles City within 70 minutes, assuming good driving conditions. Approximately four or five times a year it is necessary to request air ambulance helicopter service out of Billings.

Jordan Country still lacks sufficient population to support either a local optometrist or dentist. The closest optometrists are in Glasgow, Miles City, and Lewistown, from 85 to 130 miles away. The nearest dental practice is in Circle, 67 miles down Highway 200, but a fly-in dentist from Billings provides one-day-a-week service.

For rural residents of 1930, school was an isolated one-room shack, staffed by a teacher who was both difficult to obtain and reluctant to stay. Garfield County high school students attended class at one of the county's two high schools in Jordan and Cohagen. Both maintained dormitories for students who lived too far away to commute on a daily basis.

During the 1980-81 school year, 13 Garfield County rural schools offered grades one through eight. Twelve were one-room school houses with enrollments ranging from three to nine and averaging less than five students. Shacks and log-cabin school houses of Bowman's time have given way to trailers and portable modular buildings which are easily adaptable to changing enrollment patterns. It is still difficult to find teachers to serve in more isolated schools where their only contact with other people might be two or three young kids for weeks on end.

Although an extensive school bus system now links many parts of Garfield County with the high school in Jordan, large sections are still beyond the service area. To accommodate these students, the county maintains a dormitory in Jordan. Built in the 1930s, this is the last public high school dormitory in the state.

The already sparse population of Garfield County has declined even more. At the time of Bowman's visit the county was home to 4,252 people. Fifty years later that figure had dropped to 1,649. Even more dramatically, during the same period the number of farms and ranches plummeted from 1,077 to 269 and the average size ballooned from 1,095 acres to 7,636.

Today, except for the Blackfoot area in northwestern Garfield County where better soil conditions permit a greater cropping emphasis, Jordan Country is primarily ranching country. Most ranchers do grow some crops and the proportion varies from none to fairly extensive small grain operations. Ranchers with little cropping land tend to have the largest operations in terms of acres. Since carrying capacity of county range averages 25 to 30 acres per head of cattle, and some sections drop as low as six head per section, ranches may spread over more than 100 square miles. The largest ranch totals just over 229 square miles of deeded and leased land.

One contemporary aspect of Jordan Country agriculture would almost certainly concern Bowman. This is the large-scale expansion of block farming. Tens of thousands of acres of former range, some of it wisely abandoned as unsuitable for cropping when homesteaders fled the area beginning in the late Teens, has been broken and planted in wheat, much of it in continuous blocks thousands of acres in size. Using newer large machinery, small hills and gullies are all cultivated. The result is often a sea of ground laid bare, as far as the eye can see. "It gives me a cold feeling in the pit of my stomach," said one local in response to this latest farming fad. Others think such abuse of the land should be illegal and shudder at the thought of a series of dry, windy years and the potential for wholesale soil erosion. Bowman saw major experimentation as a part of a pioneering agricultural area. Perhaps the substantial expansion of block farming suggests that major experimentation in Jordan Country has not yet ceased.

Block farming can leave a sea of ground laid bare, and
long-time residents fear the resulting erosion in a series of
dry, windy years.

Above: *Garfield County High School, Jordan, maintains the last public school dormitory in the state.* — John Alwin

Below: *The Burlington Northern spur which terminates at Brockway 55 miles east of Jordan is as close as a rail approaches to Jordan Country. Next rail service to the west is Lewistown, 130 miles away.* — John Alwin

Above: *Box Elder Creek east of Winnett. —* Mark Thompson

Right: *Residents of Jordan country make good use of the Hell Creek Recreation area on an arm of Fort Peck Reservoir.* — Mark Thompson

Right: *Downtown Jordan. A ticket will not get you there — no train, bus, or plane makes connections,* **Below Top:** *but it is no desert, these generous fields are North of Jordan,* **Bottom:** *Range west of Jordan.* — John Alwin, Mark Thompson, Mark Thompson

JORDAN

You can't really say you've seen Eastern Montana until you've been to Jordan. This little town of 500 has lent its name to the surrounding sparsely populated area of Jordan Country. Since the region is without a through north-south highway and the state's two major east-west routes are far to the north and south, chances are you've never been there unless you happened to make a wrong turn!

State highway department statistics show that Highway 200 passing east-west through Jordan, and Highway 22 linking it with Miles City, are among the state's least traveled paved highways. Travelers seem to avoid passing through Jordan Country for fear that there will be no restaurants, gas stations, or accommodations. It is true that a "Big Mac attack" cannot be satisfied in Jordan, but the community has several good cafes and bars (even a combination liquor store/barbershop), a selection of gas stations, and the Garfield Motel and others provide pleasant accommodations.

The community recognizes its relative isolation and the Garfield County Commercial Club even plays it up in their promotional brochure on Jordan in which they claim it is "the most isolated frontier town in the United States."

Jordan's isolation and its vestiges of the Old West have received national press coverage. Paul Harvey mentioned the Wild West aspect of the community on his February 18, 1981, national radio show. A recent Associated Press wire service story entitled, "Reach, Pilgrim" and datelined Jordan, Montana, clearly identifies the region with a John Wayne syndrome. The report relates how the sheriff staked out the town's only drug store anticipating a robbery. Two out-of-state men were eventually captured with the help of a 30-man posse composed of members of the volunteer fire department and patrons who streamed out of a town bar.

Jordan's downtown, with false front buildings more than 70 years old, has changed surprisingly little over the decades. Even the office building of the town's first doctor who arrived in 1916 still stands abandoned on the main street. Recent progressive additions have included a supermarket, feed mill, and meat-packing plant.

Seismic crews are now a common sight in Jordan. At this time the result of their exploration is still uncertain. The community has been poised more than once before for swift and dramatic change that would put Jordan on the map. Earlier this century it was expected to evolve into the metropolis for a western corn belt. Few Jordanites would be surprised if major change continues to evade their community.

YELLOWSTONE COUNTRY

This is the largest and most varied of our Eastern Montana regions. Here the mix of natural landscapes is unrivaled: fragile alpine tundra high atop the Pryors and Bighorns, wierdly contorted badlands, seemingly endless short grass and sage-brush-mantled prairie, picturesque ponderosa-studded hills, the dramatic gorge of the Bighorn River and the more subdued, verdant and sinuous course of the majestic Yellowstone.

This latter river lends its name to the region, which includes a sliver of area to its north and the big country drained by its major tributaries on the south. This long has been an area of ranches and irrigated farming, and they are still dominant, but Yellowstone Country is also now evolving as an energy district of national importance, rich in coal, oil and gas. Energy development has brought swift and dramatic change to the regional geography and sparked controversy as the diverse elements of agriculture and energy come together.

Range is still dominant over most of Yellowstone Country, accounting for up to 90 percent of land in farms in some counties. Large ranches which have been in families for generations are sometimes the only evidence of human habitation over broad stretches. Most ranches in the region are cow-calf operations which produce young animals for shipment to out-of-state feedlots, especially Corn Belt states. For years Iowa has been the number one destination for these cattle. Ranchers characteristically run commercial herds, although there is increasing interest in the more exotic breeds. Only in the extreme southeast, in Carter County, are cattle outnumbered by sheep.

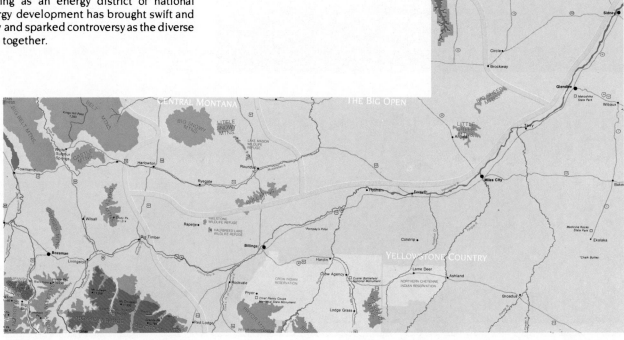

High School students from Carter County might attend school in Buffalo or Belle Fourche, South Dakota or Broadus in Powder River County. It's not that the county's single high school at Ekalaka is inadequate, it's just that the southern and northern parts of the county are not linked by paved highway.

Many of these yonland ranches are really quite isolated. High school ranch children in southern Carter County attend schools in Buffalo or Belle Fourche, South Dakota; or in Broadus, in neighboring Powder River County. It's not that the county's single high school at Ekalaka is inadequate, it's just that the southern and northern parts of the county are still not linked by paved highway. In other large, thinly populated counties, students from outlying ranches routinely board with friends or relatives, as do the numerous high school students in Custer County who live in Miles City during weekdays, but return to the ranch on weekends.

In some areas of Yellowstone Country conditions are suitable for dryland grain farming, especially in portions of northern Stillwater, western Yellowstone, Big Horn, Wibaux and Fallon counties. These are largely wheat producing regions and strip cropping gives them the characteristic striped landscape so prevalent in the Triangle and Northeast. Here, too, occasional grain elevators tower above the prairie.

Above: *Greenery south of Wibaux.* — Robert Scherting

Left: *Cash Way truck stop near Broadus.* — John Alwin

> Irrigation gives the land such a lush look, people sometimes incorrectly assume that these valley areas must receive more precipitation than adjacent range.

On the fertile alluvial soils, astride the Yellowstone and its major tributaries, the Clarks Fork of the Yellowstone, Bighorn, Tongue and Powder, irrigated farming prevails. Brown gives way to green abruptly in these irrigated districts where corn, sugar beets, hay and small grains are dominant crops. Irrigation gives the land such a lush look, people sometimes incorrectly assume that these valley areas must receive more precipitation than adjacent range. Agriculture is on a different scale here, and is much more intensive. A beet-corn farmer outside of Laurel, for instance, might operate on only 200 acres, in contrast to some Yellowstone Country ranches that exceed 100,000 acres.

Sugar beets produced in these valleys are processed at mills in Sidney and Billings. From October through February at the Great Western Sugar factory in Billings, more than 500,000 tons of beets are processed into about 200 million pounds of refined sugar. Bulk sugar is shipped as far as Chicago. Beet pulp left after refining is ideal cattle feed and is used extensively in the region. Almost all the corn grown in these valleys is cut for silage. Additional hay and barley production means an abundance of cattle feed, some of which is consumed in Yellowstone Valley feedlots. These tend to be "backgrounding" operations where young animals are given initial weight gains as opposed to final finishing prior to slaughter.

Yellowstone Country is also coal country. Eastern Montana may have 50 billion tons of surface mineable coal, both lignite and higher BTU sub-bituminous grades. Much of the better grade coal lies within Yellowstone Country. Surface strip mining is the standard method used to remove coal in the region. With this type of mining the material overlying the coal seams (overburden) is removed, usually with mammoth draglines, exposing the underlying coal. Seams are essentially flat lying, which makes mining easier, and range in thickness up to 50 feet. Since the ratio of overburden to thickness of coal seams is often small, these are among the most efficient mines in the world. Using draglines and large shovels and trucks, individual miners can produce up to 160 tons per day, many times that of counterparts in Appalachian mines. An added plus is the generally low sulfur content of this western coal, usually a half to a third that of Eastern U.S. coal, which means it is less polluting when burned.

Tongue River south of Ashland. — Jim Romo

> The state's coal production, almost all of it from Yellowstone Country, rose from 3 million tons in 1970 to almost 32.5 million tons in 1979.

Large-scale, surface strip mining in Eastern Montana began in earnest in the early 1970s. This is graphically reflected in state coal production figures (almost all from Yellowstone Country) which show a rise of from 3 million tons in 1970 to almost 32.5 million tons in 1979. Most was produced from several large strip mines in southcentral Yellowstone Country and was shipped via unit trains to Midwestern utilities under long-term contracts.

Since 1979 Eastern Montana coal production actually has declined, dropping to less than 30 million tons in 1980 and levelling off in 1981. There are numerous factors that help explain why the boom hasn't continued into the early 1980s.

Although not universally accepted as a contributing factor is Montana's coal severance tax. When Montana's 30 percent tax was initiated in 1975, Montana and Wyoming each were producing approximately 22 million tons annually. Wyoming's state coal tax is about half that of Montana's and by 1980 Wyoming production grew to 94 million tons while Montana's was less than 30 million. It seems obvious that Montana's coal severance tax has been at least a factor in the disparity of production, although the degree of influence is open to debate, as are the relative benefits and costs of a slower growth in mine production.

Another factor in the slowdown in Montana coal production relates to the general softness of the coal market. Americans are becoming more energy conscious. This is reflected in the Minnesota service area for Northern States Power where some Montana coal is burned. Demand for new electrical energy there is now growing at the rate of less than 2 percent per year in contrast to a 7 percent clip in the early '70s.

A YELLOWSTONE COUNTRY COAL MINE— WESTMORELAND RESOURCES' ABSALOKA

Like most other Yellowstone Country mines, Westmoreland Resources, Inc.'s Absaloka coal mine in northern Big Horn County is a surface strip mining operation that produces low sulfur, sub-bituminous grade coal, primarily for shipment out of the state via unit trains.

Construction at the mine site began in 1972. The first unit train was loaded on July 1, 1974 and headed for the Minneapolis/St. Paul area via a new 36-mile railroad spur along Sarpy Creek. Overburden averages 60 feet, and below that there is a total thickness of 58 feet of coal in five seams in the next 120 to 130 feet. This works out to approximately 98,000 tons of coal per surface acre, which is better than some other regional mines. In 1981 the Absaloka's 130 employees produced 5 million tons of coal and the average hourly employee earned a healthy $32,892, plus fringe benefits. Since the coal rights in this Ceded Area north of the Crow Indian Reservation still belong to the Crow Tribe, an agreement stipulates that 50 percent of the work force be tribal members and the company must pay the tribe an 8 percent royalty.

Virtually all of Westmoreland Resources coal moves by unit trains to Midwestern utility companies. Each 100-car train is loaded in four hours at the mine and unloaded at its destination with the same speed. Northern States Power of Minneapolis/St. Paul, the largest customer, purchases 3 million tons annually. Trains make the round-trip between Sarpy Creek and the Twin Cities in an amazing three days — faster than first class mail!

Five other Midwestern utilities have long-term contracts for Westmoreland Resources coal: Dairyland Power Cooperative of LaCrosse, Wisconsin; Interstate Power Company of Dubuque, Iowa; Wisconsin Power and Light of Madison, Wisconsin; Central Illinois Light Company of Peoria, Illinois; and Upper Peninsula Generating Company of Marquette, Michigan. According to Joe Presley, President of Westmoreland Resources, Inc., the Absaloka mine has a capacity of twice its present production, but the company is unable to find additional major customers.

A unit coal train, 100 cars each loaded with 100 tons, snakes across the Montana prairie. — John Alwin

Left: *Near the pictograph caves southeast of Billings.* — George Maas

Below: *Makoshika State Park.* — Jim Romo

Migrant worker's children outside Laurel. The migrant's hard labor and low wages combined with an excellent educational program will discourage migrant children from continuing as field workers. — John Alwin

SUGAR BEET MIGRANTS

Sugar beets require a lot of manual labor. Machines have helped, but hands are still needed to thin and weed the irrigated beet fields that thrive in Eastern Montana's Yellowstone drainage from Bridger to beyond Sidney. Locals don't have much interest in this back-breaking and not very well paying work, so each year around mid to late May an army of about 5,000 migrants moves into the valley to work the fields. They usually stay until early July and then disappear seemingly overnight.

Most are Mexican-Americans and at least 80 percent come north out of Texas, many from the Rio Grande Valley of south Texas. Growers often hire workers, usually an extended family, who return each year to work the same fields. It is often a phone call from a beet farmer to his workers in places like Donna or Crystal City, Texas, that starts a family on their annual trek northward.

Migrants try to arrive after planting, when young beets are about two inches tall and ready for thinning. Planting by machine works fine for getting beets in rows 20 to 24 inches apart, but machines invariably plant beets too close together within their individual rows. Using hoes, migrants work their way through fields thinning rows so plants are about nine inches apart, approximately the width of a hoe. Some growers are now using electronic-eye thinning machines, but these can't be used if spring rains make fields muddy.

Ten days to two weeks after thinning, weeds have usually sprouted and migrants return to the fields with their hoes. Cultivators are used to remove weeds between rows, but cannot be used any closer than within a few inches of the beets. This leaves a narrow strip near the plants which is the responsibility of the field workers. Workers sometimes have to return for a final hand weeding in another two weeks.

Wages paid to workers are agreed upon by oral contract before the thinning begins. Planters usually pay a total price per acre for both thinning and weeding. An average, combined per-acre figure ranges from $40 to $55. When the thinning machine is used first, workers might get only about half the normal thinning rate to clean up after the machine.

Good workers can make more than $1,000 during the two-month season in Montana, but for most families, an average income would be between $500 and $750 per worker. Migrants talk of times a few years ago, "before all the machines" when higher incomes were possible. Even 15-year-old Maria Guerrero of Donna, Texas, who has been coming up to work in fields outside Laurel since age one complains that "machines are taking away all our work."

While available work has decreased, housing conditions for some migrants have improved. Still, Jim Gonzales, Executive Director of the Montana Migrant Council estimates that at least 80 percent of migrant housing in the Yellowstone drainage area is substandard. Deficiencies include no indoor plumbing, no screening, no ventilation, and extreme crowding, sometimes with six or more people per sleeping room. Grossly inadequate housing is an acute problem in the energy-boom areas around Sidney and Fairview where demands for housing by oil industry workers leave little available for seasonal migrants.

It is becoming increasingly difficult to find young people among these hard-working families who plan to continue the migrant way of life as adults. Education provides the opportunity for change and many school-age children enroll in the federally funded Migrant Education Program. Available to all ages, it allows children through high school to make up classes they miss while away for part of the school year. Typical of many of the younger migrants, Maria says she is not going to work in the fields the rest of her life. Her mother is encouraging her to become a secretary, but she wants to be a nurse.

Once Maria and her family finish in the Montana beet fields, they head south to the farms of West Texas where they hoe cotton for about six weeks before returning home to Donna. Other migrants leave the Yellowstone and move east to pick cucumbers or tomatoes in Michigan, Ohio and Wisconsin before returning to their southern homes.

The nomadic life of these migrants is a difficult one, but 20-year-old Josefina Guerrero, Maria's sister-in-law, says "It's exciting, fun, boring, and we're all happy."

Above Left: *Dean Bangert harvests corn on his 1,600-acre farm outside Hysham. Of farming he says, "You've got to get bigger or you ain't going to exist."* — John Alwin
Below: *South of Rockvale irrigated sugar beets and corn fields fill in the valley floor of the Clark's Fork of the Yellowstone, while dryland grain crops occupy the bench.* — John Alwin

Above: *The Hay Creek School north of Alzada.* — John Alwin

MONTANA'S COAL SEVERANCE TAX

Unlike trees, coal is a non-renewable resource; once coal is dug up and consumed, it is gone for good. The coal severance tax was designed, in part, to assure that benefits reaped from exploitation by today's Montanans are shared with future residents.

Montana has taxed state coal production since 1921, when a rate of 5¢ per ton was imposed. Since then, the rates have ranged from 4¢ to 40¢ per ton. The Montana state legislature enacted the current severance tax in 1975. Actual tax rate depends on the coal's BTU (heat) content and the method of extraction (surface or underground).

In 1982 there were nine operating coal mines in the state. The two operations in the Bull Mountains do not pay any severance tax since they produce less than 20,000 tons annually, and the Knife River mine, which produces lignite coal for a coal-fired power plant at Savage in Richland County, pays only 20 percent of the contract sale price because of that coal's lower BTU value. The state's six other producing mines, all within Yellowstone Country and all surface mines, produce coal with a heat value of at least 9,000 BTUs per pound and, therefore, pay the maximum 30 percent, or about $2.30 per ton.

Fifty percent of all coal-tax revenues are held in a permanent trust. The interest from this constitutional trust fund may be appropriated by the legislature each session, but the principle cannot be "touched" unless three-fourths of the members of each house vote in favor of its appropriation. A total of 8.75 percent is allocated to assist impacted areas in dealing with costs associated with required new schools, water and sewer lines, street repairs and fire equipment. The remainder of the tax is distributed to the state's general fund (19 percent), and statewide programs including an educational trust fund (10 percent), school equalization (5 percent), parks, arts, and aesthetics (2.5 percent), alternative energy grants (2.25 percent), and smaller amounts to renewable resource development, land-use planning, water development, and libraries.

Montana has been attacked by coal companies and Congressional delegates from some of the states where Montana coal is consumed for having what they see as an excessively high state coal tax, claiming it is an impediment to interstate commerce. As supporters of the tax point out, Montana's is consistent with taxes other states impose on their natural resources. In fact, Montana's $75 million a year revenue seems a mere pittance compared to the $1.5 *billion* Texas collects each year from its severence tax (mostly on oil and gas), or the more than $500 million taken in each year by Louisiana and Alaska. In fact, Montana ranked ninth in the nation in 1980 for state severance tax collections.

Montana's Congressional delegation has aptly defended the tax, pointing out that it adds only a few cents a week to the utility bills of out-of-state customers who consume electricity produced by burning Montana coal. Much more significant is the transportation cost factor, which can triple the price of coal once it leaves the mine.

The United States Supreme Court has upheld Montana's right to set its coal severance tax rate under existing legislation. But the battle to retain this important legislation has not yet been won. Congressional action, which could limit coal-severance taxes to 12.5 percent, is sure to resurface. Such a ceiling would cost Montana about $40 million per year at current levels of production.

Raising funds at the grass roots — as in this auction — the Northern Plains Resource Council has had remarkable influence in the state's political affairs — Courtesy, Northern Plains Resource Council.

THE NORTHERN PLAINS RESOURCE COUNCIL

They've squared off against some of the world's largest multinationals, this interesting amalgam of young environmental activists, farmers, ranchers and citizens concerned about mineral and other developments in the Northern Great Plains. Formed in 1972, the organization brought together grass-roots groups of farmers and ranchers in southeast and southcentral Montana who were concerned with strip mining and mine-mouth power plants and the effects they would have on water and air quality, crop yields, local populations, roads, schools and a traditional rural lifestyle.

Northern Plains Resource Council staffer Margaret MacDonald considers the organization "kind of a hybrid Populist-type movement." Dues-paying membership has grown to 1,500. Annual dues of $15, individual cash contributions of $1,000 and more, fund raisers like spaghetti dinners and auctions of donated items, including art and antiques have built the group's war chest. Today Northern Plains is one of the most vocal and influential forces on Eastern Montana's environmental scene.

The council maintains a full-time staff of 12 among its main office in Billings and field offices in Glendive and Helena. They provide local groups with guidance and information, staff services and access to experts and a statewide network of supporters. Through their monthly newsletter, *The Plains Truth*, they keep their membership current on developments that may have implications for the region.

The organization has taken a stand on numerous environmental issues including the Colstrip-area mines and mine-mouth power plants, Tenneco's plans for a coal gasification plant in Wibaux County, Burlington Northern's possible Circle West synfuel plant at Circle. It is currently fighting mines within a several-hundred-square-mile zone in the Tongue River Valley and the construction of an 82-mile-long railroad from Miles City south along the Tongue River. In recent years the group's interest has expanded well beyond the Yellowstone Country's coal fields to include, for example, the effects of Saskatchewan coal fired power plants on irrigation waters in Northeast Montana's Poplar River Valley, potential mining activities in the Stillwater Complex of southern Stillwater County, and ultra-high voltage transmission lines in western Montana valleys.

Western coal producers, including some Montana operators, are presently lobbying against a recent amendment to the federal Clean Air Act which they see as a further threat to potential markets for low-sulfur western coal. In 1977 the Act was modified to require all new coal-fired utility plants to use "scrubbers" to control sulfur dioxide emissions, irrespective of the coal to be burned. Previously it made good economic sense for Midwestern utilities to haul in relatively low sulfur, sub-bituminous coal from Montana which they could burn without scrubbers and still meet air quality standards. Now there is less reason for a new utility plant to burn this lower BTU coal when there are much closer sources of higher grade coal. That this coal also has a much higher sulfur content is no longer the determining factor, now that pollution-control devices are mandatory on new plants.

No one would deny that expansion of mining in the decade of the 1970s has had an impact on Yellowstone Country and Eastern Montana. The difference of opinion centers around how large that impact has been and what have been the relative costs and benefits. Watchdog environmental groups like the Northern Plains Resource Council and well informed locals have kept coal operators honest and current legislation helps assure a fairly regulated industry. It may even be that with present legislation and at present levels of production coal mining may not be the number one threat to Eastern Montana's environment.

> One farmer/speculator can tear up and lay bare in one year more acreage by block farming than all the acreage disturbed by strip mining in Eastern Montana to date.

According to the state Department of Lands, a total of 7,918 acres of Eastern Montana's 64 million acres (1/100th of 1 percent of the region) has been, or is now under permit to be disturbed by surface strip mining. Obviously both the environmental and socio-economic impacts of large-scale coal mining extend beyond the limits of the disturbed land, but there are agricultural practices that may have more profound environmental impact over much larger areas. The recent large-scale expansion of block farming in Eastern Montana may have grave consequences for the state and region. One farmer/speculator can tear up and lay bare more acreage in one year than all the acreage disturbed by strip mining in Eastern Montana to date. Without an environmental impact statement, permits, or bonds, this individual can significantly modify the environment in such a way as to threaten serious loss of soil to wind and water erosion. Air quality can be lowered, streams polluted, and local wildlife impacted. Likewise, current summer fallow practices have been linked to saline seep which has already taken more land out of production than strip mining of coal could in decades, even without any reclamation.

Coal-related development does have the potential to remake the geography of Yellowstone Country and other sections of Eastern Montana. The greatest potentials for change may lie in a significant expansion of strip mines, and of mine-mouth power plants which burn Eastern Montana coal and ship power out of the region by extra-high voltage transmission lines. The 1971 North Central Power Study, which identified 22 Eastern Montana sites suitable for a massive coal-fired generator of from 1,000 to 5,000 megawatts, startled many, but we have yet to see any indication that the study was a prognosticator of future developments.

A major complex of synfuel plants also could impact the region massively. The technology already exists to create liquid and gas fuels from coal and, in fact, Nazi Germany used synthetic fuels derived from coal to help run its war effort. The Republic of South Africa gets a large part of its gasoline supply from its huge synthetic fuels industry. Here in the United States the synfuel industry is still in its infancy, and a number of potential operators are watching to see what happens with the $2.6 billion pilot Great Plains Gasification Project at Beulah, North Dakota.

Yellowstone Country now finds itself in the midst of yet another energy boom — oil and gas. This activity is centered in the eastern portion of the region which reaches into the Williston Basin. Like the Northeast and the eastern portion of the Big Open, this section of Yellowstone Country has been riding the crest of an oil/gas boom for several years.

> The Williston Basin is an oilman's utopia. In Richland County more strikes than dry holes were drilled — almost unheard of in the oil industry.

The Williston Basin is a bit of an oilman's utopia. Its relatively simple geologic structure enhances the search for oil, and for example, more strikes than dry holes were dug in Richland County — almost unheard of in the oil industry. By the late 1970s the Williston Basin was *the* wildcat area in the nation. Developments in Canada and oil deregulation here in the United States only added to the Basin's desirability. Thousands of oil immigrants caused local towns to burst at the seams. Sidney, once a quiet agricultural center, experienced a break-neck 26 percent increase in population during the decade of the 1970s.

THE MONTANA STRIP AND UNDERGROUND MINE RECLAMATION ACT

In the late 1970s, as required by federal law, Montana modified its existing coal-mining legislation to conform to new federal guidelines. Montana already had legislation of its own that was touted as being among the toughest in the nation, but changes were necessary to conform to the newly established nationwide standards.

The Montana Department of State Lands was charged with the general supervision, administration, and enforcement of the new act. Coal operators intending to open either surface or underground mines must first obtain a permit from State Lands. Permit applications must include a detailed plan for the mining, reclamation, revegetation, and rehabilitation of the land and water that would be affected by the mining operation. A long list of specific information is required, including the name and date of the daily newspaper of dominant circulation within the county in which the applicant has prominently announced an application for a mine permit and clearly located the area of the proposed mine.

Before a permit will be issued, the operator must post a bond, or security deposit, payable to the state of Montana, of not less than $200 per acre of land that would be affected by the mine. The deposit is adjusted to reflect the degree of disturbance and the cost of reclamation. Bonds have ranged as high as $12,000 to $16,000 per acre.

Once all requirements have been met, an operator may begin mining. Excavation begins with the removal of topsoil and its storage in a manner that guards against erosion and pollution. Once coal is removed, the law stipulates that the land surface be regraded and "restored to the approximate original contour." Operators are also required to restore the land in such a way that it can be used in the same manner, or if reasonably possible, in a better way, than it was used prior to excavation.

As successful reclamation proceeds, portions of the security bond may be released. The final portion of the bond cannot be returned until a diverse, effective, and permanent vegetative cover capable of self-regeneration has been established on disturbed lands. Ideally a plant community of the same seasonal variety native to the area is to be re-established, but approved introduced species may be used. Revegetated areas have to pass three critical tests: 1) must be able to withstand the same grazing pressure as prior to mining, 2) must be able to regenerate under natural conditions that can include drought, heavy snow, and strong winds, and 3) must be able to prevent soil erosion to at least the extent as the vegetation prior to mining.

As of early 1982, no bonds or portions of bonds have been released for reclamation/revegetation. Since ten years must elapse between the last seeding, fertilizing, and irrigating and the return of the remaining bond, it is premature to expect release of any bonds for areas that were initially disturbed in the early to mid 1970s.

Left: *Don Johnson, a floor hand, yellow hat; Lori Price, motorist, overalls; and Jon Haugen in white shirt tend the pipe under the eye of Don Paraswchuk, driller. This Canadian rig was scheduled to drill to 12,500 feet.* — John Alwin

Right: *the new crop in the sugar beet field is an oil derrick.* — John Alwin

SYNFUEL PLANTS IN EASTERN MONTANA

In a July 12, 1979 U.S. Department of Energy report entitled *Environmental Analysis of Synthetic Liquid Fuels*, it was noted that ten Eastern Montana counties met siting requirements (coal, water, non-stringent air quality standards) for at least one 100,000-barrel-per-day (BPD) plant. Six of the counties could support an even larger 300,000-BPD facility.

Any one of these would be the largest synfuel plant in the nation. A 100,000-BPD plant would employ 3,000 workers in the facility and in the supporting mining activities. According to this government study, the total potential population increase with this level of new jobs could be expected to reach 20,000 in rural areas. To build just ten of the smaller plants could mean 200,000 new residents for Eastern Montana — equal to 50 percent of the present population. The boom-town syndrome would be profound since many of the *counties* now have populations of less than 5,000.

Residents can hope only that many serious questions will be answered before the geography of the state's eastern two-thirds is remade. What is to become of the communities once the 20- to 40-year lifetime of the plants expires? How much ground will be disturbed by strip mining and how much will be reclaimed effectively? How will farmers be compensated for weight loss in the wheat owing to air pollution? What are the long-term global consequences of heightened carbon dioxide generation associated with burning synthetic fuels produced from coal? How will the huge quantities of waste by handled? Is there really sufficient water?

Tenneco Coal's proposed synthetic fuel plant in the far eastern portion of Montana may become the state's first large-scale synfuel complex. The preferred site is six miles southeast of Wibaux. Present plans call for the first synthetic fuel to be produced in 1990. It is expected that during construction peak, as many as 4,000 would be employed, and during later operation, employment could total approximately 1,050 in the plant and 300 in the associated coal mine. When in full operation the plant would consume 13,500,000 tons of lignite coal per year, just under half of Montana's current annual production, to produce 280,000,000 cubic feet of syngas which would be carried to Midwest markets through the Northern Border Pipeline. During its lifespan the mine would remove coal from under a 28-square-mile area. Tenneco projects that during the peak of construction regional population would increase by 13,000, then stabilize at a net gain of 6,000 new regional residents. Wibaux County had a 1980 population of approximately 1,500.

Speaking before the United States Senate on November 7, 1979, Montana Senator Max Baucus warned that the impact from synfuel development on Montana was potentially massive and pointed out that "Montana . . . will feel the burden of synthetic fuels because our water — the lifeblood of our economy — would be threatened, our air potentially polluted, and our communities bursting into boom towns. But even if I were not from a synfuel state, I would make these arguments, because only unwise national policy produces such economics and environmental consequences."

BILLINGS

Already home to more than one of every ten Montanans, metropolitan Billings is astir with growth and development. During the decade of the 1970s the area accounted for almost 25 percent of Montana's new residents. The Magic City is now the state's largest, and its rich and sprawling 200,000-square-mile hinterland reaches well beyond Montana's borders claiming large swaths in both Wyoming and North Dakota. It contains one of the world's largest coal reserves, active oil and gas fields and millions of acres of agricultural land. The final quarter of the 20th century is witnessing the ascendance of Billings to the position of undisputed hub of this burgeoning northern plains region — just as its promoters predicted a century ago.

Billings is one of a string of railroad-spawned communities which sprang up along the Northern Pacific as it snaked through the Yellowstone Valley in 1881-82. The namesake of Northern Pacific President, Frederick Billings, the community was designated division point on the new line. Finally, a direct rail link with the outside world and distant markets meant that this resource-rich region could be tapped. Promoters billed their new town as the "Denver of the Northwest" and were confident it would become the focal point in the evolving prairie north. Enough city lots for a town of 25,000 were surveyed and sold to speculators as far away as New York City, and a town sprouted almost overnight.

Billings was not the first community to take root on the banks below the majestic Rimrocks. The earliest "town" in the vicinity was a place called Coulson, after the steamboat company whose craft navigated both the Missouri and Yellowstone. Around 1876 Perry J. McAdow built a general store on the north bank of the Yellowstone near where the Burlington Northern bridge now spans the river.

McAdow and another man also operated a ferry crossing and within a year the town of Coulson had developed.

Coulson served as a stage station, steamboat landing, stop-over point for travelers, and as trading center for the early farmers and ranchers in the Yellowstone Country. By 1882 the town boasted several general stores, a blacksmith shop, restaurants, a hotel and no less than five saloons.

Coulson continued as the focus of the region until the coming of the railroad. In anticipation of its arrival, a townsite was surveyed and residents of the six-year-old community were more confident than ever of their town's future. But Coulson's hopes were dashed when the railroad's townsite company decided lot prices were too high, went two miles west, and platted their own town of Billings. In 1883 a street railway linked the two communities, but the new rival soon eclipsed its predecessor.

Billings grew up in the Wild West era and its early history is peppered with the colorful characters of the time. One of these was John Johnson (sometimes Johnston), also known as "Liver-Eating" Johnson. His fame as a mountain man and scout recently was popularized in the Hollywood film, "Jeremiah Johnson," starring Robert Redford. According to legend his nickname originated from his taking bites from the liver of Crow Indians he killed. In his *The Plainsmen of the Yellowstone*, Mark Brown traces the peculiar nickname to an 1869 incident at the mouth of the Musselshell when, while awaiting the arrival of a steamboat, Johnson and his fellow trappers were attacked by a Sioux war party. The trappers were victorious, and after the battle Johnson allegedly cut out the liver of a warrior and ate part of it. Johnson always claimed he only pretended to take a bite, and even though his story was corroborated by a "reliable witness" the nickname stuck.

Hauling Beets to Sugar Factory, Billings, Mont.

By the late 1870s mountain men like Johnson who chose to remain on the frontier had to take up new careers. In a turnabout of professions, "Liver-Eating" took up law enforcement. He was a physically powerful man with a reputation to match, ideal qualities for law officers of the time. The lure of quick riches and easy money attracted an unsavory lot of fast-buck artists, gamblers and general undesirables to Coulson, Billings and other western frontier towns, places where the sheriffs had to be just as ornery. Johnson was evidently well suited to his job as deputy sheriff at Coulson, maintaining law and order without a jail.

If one knows where to look, reminders of Billings' earlier times can be picked out of the modern landscape. Just west of town is the site of the 1823 Jones and Immel Massacre. That spring a group of 30 Missouri Fur Company men under these two leaders was ambushed by a large Blackfeet war party. The men were returning to their post at the mouth of the Big Horn River and were heavily laden with pelts after a successful stint in the vicinity of the Three Forks of the Missouri. Indians made off with more than half the furs, all the horses, and left both Jones and Immel and four other trappers dead. The incident forced the company to withdraw permanently from the Yellowstone Country.

On the east side of Billings overlooking the Yellowstone is an obvious sandstone bluff known as Sacrifice Cliff. According to legend, in 1837 many Indians afflicted with smallpox leapt from the precipice either to end their misery or to appease their gods. Others were placed there after their death. Legend has it that two young men rode a white horse off the cliff, offering themselves in exchange for an end to the smallpox epidemic devastating their people. To this date, Crow tradition records that their effort succeeded.

Four miles northeast of Billings is the site of Major Eugene Baker's camp, which was attacked by a party of Sioux in the summer of 1872. Major Baker was in command of the several hundred soldiers who were to protect the west-end Northern Pacific Railroad Survey Party. Marauding Sioux evidently happened upon the camp by accident and decided to steal the cavalry horses and wagon mules. They were unsuccessful and may have lost more than the 40 warriors they did if Major Baker had not been in a drunken stupor in his tent at the time, unable to take command of his troops.

Even though 1982 marks Billings' centennial, the town still has landmarks dating from its youth. Most residents know about their community's own Boot Hill Cemetery atop the Rimrocks. In many ways this cemetery with its shallow graves is typical of pioneer graveyards. Those buried there include well known Indian scout, Yellowstone Kelly, who served as guide and interpreter for Colonel Nelson A. Miles in the Indian campaigns of the 1870s. Perhaps the most notable personality laid to rest in Billings' Boot Hill was "Muggins" Taylor, the scout who carried the first news of the Custer Battle to the outside world.

Time and progress have taken their toll on most of Billings' early structures, but some remain as vestiges of earlier times. Adaptive re-use should help assure their continued existence as touchstones in Billings' rich heritage. Begun in 1899 and completed in 1901, the two-story Parmly Billings Memorial Library still stands and is now listed in the National Register of Historic Places. Located at 2822 Montana Avenue, the building was given to the city as a gift from Frederick Billings, Jr. He financed the building as a memorial to his brother, Parmly Billings, who was active in the town's business community. The structure now houses the Western

1909 post card. — Courtesy,
Len Eckel

Heritage Center with its displays of Old West paintings and artifacts and numerous other displays and collections.

At 301 North 27th Street is another local landmark listed in the National Register. The building was completed in 1910 as a home for the local Elks Club. In 1918 ownership passed to the Billings Chamber of Commerce after the Elks realized they could no longer afford to maintain the expensive structure. The Chamber moved out in 1970 and a private corporation of interested residents purchased it. The building now houses offices.

The historic core of Billings developed along Montana Avenue north of the railroad tracks. Today this portion of the central business district, with its ornate late 19th century buildings, is within the nationally registered Billings Historic District. The designated area is bordered by North 21st and 26th Streets, First Avenue North and the tracks.

Many of Billings' wealthy residents built substantial homes in the fashionable Westside District shortly after the turn of the century. This neighborhood, bounded by Division Street and 5th Street West, and between Grand Avenue and Broadwater, allowed the community's well-healed to live away from the noise and congestion of the central city just to the east and yet to be only a short commuting distance from the town's commercial center.

Most homes in this neighborhood were built between 1903 and 1920. Some are veritable mansions, like the residence at 914 Division Street. This imposing three-story French Gothic home was built in 1902-03 by Preston B. Moss, one of Montana's wealthiest men. This was the home of the family that built Billings' equally historic Northern Hotel in 1903 and the present Northern in 1942 after fire destroyed the original. The home's exterior walls are of reddish-brown Lake Superior sandstone and the foundation was built using sandstone block from the Rimrocks. The glass conservatory, like the entire structure, is all original. The home still is occupied by the Moss family.

The Castle, as it is locally known, at 622 North 29th Street, outside of the historic Westside District is probably the most distinctive older home in all of Billings. Some say owner Austin North built the medieval-like structure in 1903 simply to lure the community's wealthy into investing in his new subdivision. With its crow-stepped gable, steep pitched roof and round turret capped by a battlement, it looks strangely out of place. Today the home serves as a museum/art gallery with apartments on the upper two floors.

Economic growth and prosperity that catapulted Billings into prominence during the first part of this century have been renewed. Michael Skaggs, Director of Economic Development for the Billings Area Chamber of Commerce, points out that "Billings is on the verge of some growth that has never been seen in this part of the country." His office projects that metropolitan Billings will grow to more than 140,000 by 1990 and may well reach 175,000 by the year 2000. *Money* magazine recently included Billings in its list of ten small American cities (in the 50,000 to 250,000 population range) with "Big Futures."

Much of the recent growth can be linked to energy — coal, oil and natural gas. Major mines and producing fields are at least a two-hour drive out of the city, and even though some blue-collar energy workers live in town and commute to work, Billings is more of a white-collar energy town. Scores of energy related companies have set up offices in Billings, and more seem to arrive almost daily.

The Billings area's economic muscle and stability go beyond energy. The community has the distinction of having the most varied economic base of any urban center in the state. Important sectors include wholesale and retail trade, (a reflection of its role as regional trade center), federal government employment, (including the U.S. Bureau of Reclamation, U.S. Bureau of Land Management, and U.S. Forest Service), manufacturing (especially processing of agricultural commodities grown in surrounding areas), oil refining (at three refineries), and transportation (mostly railroad workers). Billings clearly is not a one-industry town.

Billings also is home to two fine colleges. Rocky Mountain College is a private, church-affiliated school, and Eastern Montana College is the third largest college in the state university system. EMC has grown significantly with the city and region and some now feel a full university status is appropriate.

Each year tens of thousands of city residents and other Eastern Montanans benefit from the wide variety of entertainment available in Billings. Loyal fans closely follow the progress of the town's three professional sports teams. For hockey fans it is the Billings Bighorns; basketball enthusiasts follow the Volcanoes; and the Mustangs bring exciting pro baseball to town.

Three big-purse rodeos help keep this aspect of the Old West alive and kicking. The Yellowstone Exhibition Rodeo, the Northern International Livestock Exhibition and Rodeo (NILE), and the Northern Rodeo finals annually give local cowboys a chance to compete against some of the best in the country.

As the state's largest metropolitan area, it isn't surprising that Billings has one of the state's most mixed populations. Its community of almost 2,000 American Indians is second only to Great Falls. The metro area is also home to almost one-third of Montanans of Spanish origin, and one-sixth of all Blacks in the state. Other ethnic groups contribute to this "big city" population mosaic. Chinese, Japanese, German, French, Greek, Italian and Mexican restaurants are locally popular.

Billings also has the theatre, arts and other social and cultural amenities that enhance life in the Magic City. It is easy to understand why many Billings residents who are forced to move from the city find they have a definite homing instinct. Resident Frank Messmer sums it up nicely when he points out that the community "has about everything you need . . . it's very big city-like and yet it still has the advantages of neighborliness and a strong sense of community."

COLSTRIP

Few would deny that Colstrip is an energy boom town, but it is a boom town with a difference. Unlike many other such communities in the northern Great Plains, it has avoided much of the visual blight and environmental squalor that has come to be expected of such towns.

Colstrip's boom is relatively new even though commercial coal mining there dates back more than half a century. Mining began in the 1920s when the Northern Pacific moved its operations east from Red Lodge out onto the Eastern Montana plains. Inadequate production, labor problems and expensive underground operations had convinced the company it was time to shift to the less expensively mined coal in the Colstrip area.

The N.P. laid track south from its main line in the Yellowstone Valley and shipped its first coal in 1924. Soon N.P. locomotives for hundreds of miles to both east and west burned Colstrip coal. The mine was extremely economical since workers were able to produce five times as much coal per man. By the 1950s even this relatively inexpensive coal could no longer forestall the shift to diesels, and the mine was closed.

In 1959 the Montana Power Company, through its Western Energy subsidiary, obtained a lease on area coal reserves and surface rights, as well as the townsite of Colstrip and the old mining equipment. Nine years later coal from the mine began supplying the company's 180-megawatt Corette power plant in Billings.

Things really started happening in the early 1970s when the community we know today began taking form. In 1972 the Montana Power Company and Puget Sound Power and Light began construction of two 350-megawatt, coal-fired power plants, Colstrip I and II. Colstrip I was completed in the fall of 1975 and Colstrip II came on-line in the summer of 1976. Western Energy's Colstrip operation produced more coal than could be consumed locally at I and II and at the Corette plant, and some was shipped to Midwestern utilities.

Between 1970 and 1976 population in the greater Colstrip area skyrocketed from 442 to almost 2,700 as construction workers, as well as new miners and employees of the power plants, swelled population. Almost as soon as the community had stabilized at approximately 2,000 in the late 1970s, construction of 700-megawatt Colstrip III and IV set off another boom. Within two years population rose to 5,000 and is expected to peak at 8,000 in the fall of 1982. Colstrip III and IV are scheduled for completion in 1984 and 1985, and it is projected that the community will stabilize at around 4,500 after 1985. By then Western Energy expects to be mining about 18 million tons of coal per year, about 7 million tons of which will be burned at I through IV.

Colstrip is a planned, modern community built to house coal plant workers and their families. Don't look for the "old part" of town here. It doesn't exist. — John Alwin

In the shadows of the four mammoth power plants and their towering smoke stacks is the curious town of Colstrip. This isn't a raw, dusty, mining camp. It is an unexpected splash of green in the brown-toned landscape of southern Rosebud County, a carefully planned and tidy community with wide paved streets, numerous parks and green lawns. Don't look for a "main drag" with stores and shops on both sides; there isn't one. Most business establishments are inside or adjacent to the community's enclosed shopping mall.

The visual balance of past to present is shifted here compared to other Eastern Montana towns of similar size. You have to look to find the "old" in Colstrip. Homes that were built prior to 1930 are in the minority, vastly outnumbered by suburban style ranch houses, condominiums, and innumerable mobile homes.

Montana Power has developed a visitor's center across from the shopping mall where the community's history, mine reclamation, and the story of the generating plants are explained through displays and five-minute video shorts. At the center arrangements can be made for a bus tour of area operations or, for the more independent minded, there is literature available for self-guided tours.

EKALAKA

Eighty miles south of Wibaux and Interstate 94, near the end of paved highway, is Ekalaka, the town with the rhythmic Indian name. It is Montana's only county seat not served by a through paved highway. Although still known as the town at the end of the road, this is not quite true today since pavement now continues on to the south for some 20 miles before giving way to gravel for the remaining 50-odd miles to Alzada and U.S. Highway 212.

Here in this town of 620 and county of 1,800 is one of the most extraordinary county museums in the nation. Despite an off-the-beaten-path location its dinosaur collection ranks in a class that would include the American Museum of Natural History in New York City and Pittsburgh's Carnegie Museum.

High school teacher Marshall Lambert started amassing his impressive dinosaur collection under the steam pipes in the high school basement in the 1930s. The museum now includes a wide range of artifacts and other historical items, including those of aboriginal occupants and early settlers. It has outgrown its basement location and in early 1982 was in the process of being moved to a new downtown site in an older stone building. Even in the expanded 6,000-square-foot exhibit area, the museum's locally collected dinosaurs will still hold center stage.

You'll see things here that you don't expect to see in *any* county museum. By sometime in 1983 the 35-foot-long *Anatosaurus*, a large specimen of the classic duck-billed dinosaur, will be remounted. The museum's *Triceratops*, a variety of large horned dinosaur, is ready for viewing. The *Mosasaurus*, a giant marine lizard, is being prepared for exhibition. Visitors can also see remains of the notorious *Tyrannosaurus rex*. The most unique dinosaur display is undoubtedly the skull of the Bonehead dinosaur (*Pachycephalosaurus*). There has been only one found in the world, and that was west of Ekalaka. At the time of the discovery, the museum was housed in the high school basement, hardly a place for *the* type specimen for a variety of dinosaur. Lambert wisely had the original sent to the American Museum of Natural History in New York. In return, the Carter County Museum accepted a plaster cast of the original.

Although the average visitor is probably most taken with the dinosaurs, Museum Director Lambert feels it is his rapidly expanding collection of early mammals that is paleontologically more significant. Lambert's finds from the late Cretaceous and Paleocene rocks of the area show a rapid initial evolution of mammals and the beginning of a line that has led to the subspecies, *Homo sapiens sapiens*.

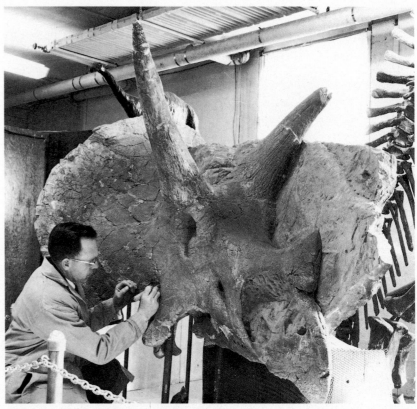

Above Left: *Downtown Ekalaka, and* **Above:** *Marshall Lambert tends a triceratops coughed up by the eastern Montana prairie.* — John Alwin, Courtesy Marshall Lambert

MILES CITY, THE CATTLE CAPITAL OF MONTANA

Miles City dates back to the late 1870s when it sprang up outside the boundary of the Fort Keogh military reservation. This post had been built in 1877, after the disastrous Custer Battle, to house troops who were charged with protecting the frontier and returning wandering bands of Indians to their reservations. Right from the start "Miles" served as a focal point for farmers and ranchers from throughout this corner of Montana. During the initial years of the open range livestock era it was a major supply center, serviced by steamships on the Yellowstone River. The arrival of the Northern Pacific Railroad in 1881 amplified its role as a center for the regional livestock industry. By 1884 the town shipped better than 200,000 head of cattle and by the summer of 1886 a half million grazed the range of a then much larger Custer County.

Miles City still has a livestock yard and ships cattle out by rail, but the relative importance of cattle to the city's economy has decreased. Today agriculture is much more diversified. Irrigated lands along the Yellowstone produce the third largest corn crop among Montana counties and tens of thousands of acres of wheat add to the agricultural mix of the Miles City hinterland.

Despite this diversification of the regional agricultural base and the fact that Miles is now a modern western town of about 10,000 which serves as educational, medical, transportation, cultural and entertainment center for southeastern Montana, a stroll along downtown's Main Street makes it clear that many city residents are still cowboys at heart. Western wear is pretty standard fare in all of Eastern Montana, but Miles City must claim the state's highest per capita ownership of Levi's, cowboy boots and hats, and elaborate belt buckles. Some communities have to fabricate a western image — in Miles City it's the real thing.

Each summer thousands throng to the city to attend the Eastern Montana Fair and various rodeos. The most famous event is the annual spring Miles City Bucking Horse Sale. Initially designed to show and auction rodeo stock to contractors, it has grown to a major event with an international reputation, which attracts more than 15,000 spectators. The three-day, Friday through Sunday, event is somewhat belatedly kicked off with a Saturday morning parade that draws more than three times the town's population.

At the Eastern Montana Fairground's rodeo arena local and national cowboys compete in bare-back and saddle-bronc riding on predictably unpredictable animals. Buyers watch for potential new rodeo stock and the crowd just hopes for exciting rides.

The local Jaycees have been running the Sale since the early 1950s and successfully have converted a formerly business-like event into a true community celebration. These three days are Miles City at its wildest. The town is jammed and downtown watering holes are filled to overflowing.

THIS IS KYUS COUNTRY

For a town the size of Miles City to have its own television station is unique in itself, but for that television station to be internationally renowned is another story.

The station is KYUS, and it began broadcasting in 1969 with both the lowest power and the smallest market of any TV station in the country. It still holds this distinction and serves the 212th largest of the nation's 212 TV market areas.

This one-of-a-kind station started small and remains small today. Husband and wife David and Ella Rivenes have been proprietors since the beginning and are now assisted by their 19-year-old granddaughter and two technicians/writers.

The uniqueness is apparent to viewers as soon as the power is switched on in the early morning. Most stations broadcast a rather mundane test pattern prior to beginning their broadcast day. KYUS is different. David and Ella like to place a brightly colored, battery-powered bear in front of their camera and play marching music.

During the average broadcast day KYUS carries up to five locally produced half-hour shows. Each weekday morning they assemble their own local, regional and state news for a brief five-minute newsbreak at 7:25 and half-hour news programs at 6 p.m. and 10 p.m. They pride themselves on presenting "good news" and, for example, announce local birthdays on the early evening broadcast. That program also usually includes obituaries in which an effort is made to point out the better qualities of the recently deceased.

Other locally produced programming is varied and oriented to serving and informing the community. For example, the Rivenes have a kiddies' show in which they both operate hand puppets and every Tuesday evening between 6:30 and 7 they carry a third-grade spelling bee. Up to three hours of remote broadcast per week might find them airing a local high school wrestling match or basketball game, or broadcasting a local church service.

David Rivenes claims his is the most unique television station in the world. Stories about KYUS have been carried by all three morning news shows, the "Tonight Show," and "To Tell the Truth," and many other programs and write-ups on the station have appeared in American magazines and newspapers and have even cropped up in places as far away as Austria, Germany and Australia.

Next time you're in Miles City, tune in and watch one of the most distinctive television stations in the country.

NORTHERN CHEYENNE RESERVATION

The site of the town of Lame Deer, tribal headquarters for the 3,200 residents of the Northern Cheyenne Reservation, doesn't fit most Montanan's stereotype of an Eastern Montana reservation town. It looks as though it were plucked out of somewhere in Western Montana and set down in the east. The low, tree-covered hills surround the town site as the road rollercoasters into the reservation's largest community.

In the Lame Deer cemetery are the graves of Chiefs Dull Knife and Little Wolf who heroically led a small band of Northern Cheyenne back to their homeland from exile in the Indian lands of Oklahoma following the tribe's participation in the Battle of the Little Big Horn. The tribe still calls itself the "Morning Star People," after Chief Dull Knife who was also known as Morning Star.

Created in 1884 the reservation today covers about 444,000 acres of rugged and often forested hills. Coal outcroppings and clinker visible along the highway are testament to the reservation's large coal deposits. The development of this resource and potential oil and gas is proving to be somewhat controversial among tribal members.

The presence of Dull Knife College at Lame Deer is indicative of recent changes on the reservation. Traditions are yielding to new ways. Most young people can no longer speak the Cheyenne language and many are unfamiliar with the traditions and legends of their parents and grandparents. This trend has been a source of concern for the tribe and has led them to seek methods of rekindling in young Cheyenne the knowledge and pride of their Indian ancestry.

Left: *Dull Knife College reflects Northern Cheyenne commitment to improving education — in the tribe's own setting.* **Top:** *George Harris is as proud to know the "old ways" as he is of his four years in the South Pacific during WWII as a Marine.* **Bottom:** *West of Lame Deer.* — John Alwin photos

Top: *The Custer battle plays an important part in Crow Reservation history.* **Bottom:** *On the Custer National Forest.* **Right:** *Crow children must emerge into a multi-cultural world.* — John Alwin, Jim Romo, John Alwin

CROW INDIAN RESERVATION

The original Crow Reservation dates back to 1851, when the tribe received a gigantic 38-million-acre reserve spilling over large portions of today's Montana and Wyoming. As has happened so often with other reservations, this one also shrunk with time as whites gained title to portions. By 1977 Crow trust holdings had contracted to just over 2 million acres.

Today 4,500 tribal members reside on the reservation and about one-third that number live off the reserve. Crow Agency, with a population of approximately 1,000, is the largest town and has served as tribal headquarters since 1884.

Unlike many other western reservations, the Crow's are blessed with not only a scenic and physically varied reserve, but with one having an abundance of natural resources. Much of the eastern portion is underlain by strippable coal reserves and the tribe is negotiating with Shell Oil Company in conjunction with a planned coal mine in that section. North of the reservation and south of the Yellowstone River, in the Ceded Area (ceded by the United States government in 1904), Westmoreland Resources, Inc. operates its Absaloka coal mine. The tribe receives a royalty on each ton since this coal, and that under 150,000 acres of the Ceded Area, still belong to the tribe. Oil and gas on the reservation also look promising and should add additional moneys to tribal income.

For the visitor, there are numerous recreational opportunities. One popular tourist stop is Bighorn Canyon National Monument, much of which lies within the boundaries of the reservation. Each year, even more visitors stop to see Custer Battlefield National Monument, just three miles south of Crow Agency. During the third week of August the colorful Crow Fair Celebration and Pow-Wow brings together thousands of Indians and as many as 500 tipis for, among other events, a reenactment of the Custer Battle. Off the main routes in the far west of the reservation are the home and grave of the venerable Chief Plenty Coups, preserved as a memorial state monument to this last chief of the Crows.

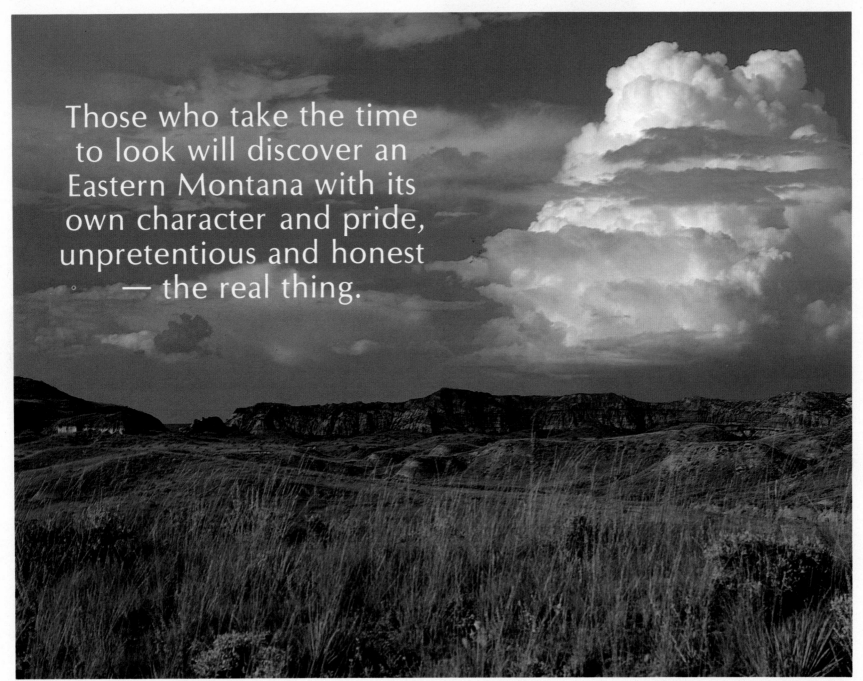

Those who take the time to look will discover an Eastern Montana with its own character and pride, unpretentious and honest — the real thing.

Thunderheads in the Powder River country, east of Miles City. — Rick Graetz

FRONT COVER PHOTOS
Top left: *West of Chester — by Rick Graetz*. Right: *Milton Hein — by John Alwin*. Lower left: *Cow Island on the Missouri — by Rick Graetz*. Center: *Square Butte from near Geraldine — by Rick Graetz*.

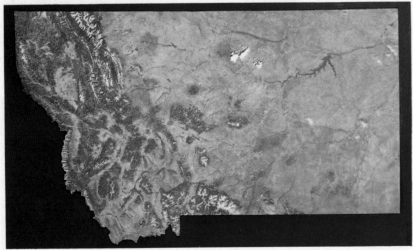

ABOUT OUR BACK COVER PHOTO
This photographic mosaic was compiled from Earth Resources Satellite Photo passes made from a height of 570 miles. It was pieced together in black and white and interpreted in color by Big Sky Magic, Larry Dodge, owner.

Commercial Color Adaptation © 1976 Big Sky Magic

This issue of Montana Geographic Series was designed by Len Visual Design, Helena, Montana.